We Give
Our Hearts to
Dogs to Tear

Bungee
"I am haunted by the ghosts of dogs…"

We Give Our Hearts to Dogs to Tear

Intimations of their Immortality

Alston Chase

Transaction Publishers
New Brunswick (U.S.A.) and London (U.K.)

Library of Congress Catalog Number: 2008001123
ISBN: 978-1-4128-0779-1
Printed in the United States of America

Library of Congress Cataloging-in-Publication Data

Chase, Alston.
    We give our hearts to dogs to tear : intimations of their immortality / Alston Chase.
        p. cm.
    ISBN 978-1-4128-0779-1
        1. Jack Russell terrier--Anecdotes. 2. Human-animal relationships--Anecdotes. 3. Chase, Alston. I. Title.

SF429.J27C43 2008
636.755--dc22

                                                                2008001123

APR   2009

For Diana, who remembers

Books by Alston Chase

Group Memory: A Guide to College and Student Survival in the 1980s, (New York: Atlantic Monthly Press, 1980).

Playing God in Yellowstone: The Destruction of America's first National Park, (New York: Atlantic Monthly Press, 1986).

In a Dark Wood: The Fight over Forests and the Myths of Nature, (Boston: Houghton Mifflin, 1995) (New Brunswick: Transaction Publishers, 2001).

Observations from the Bar (fiction, under the name of Leslie Ann Nash), (San Francisco, CA: Chronicle Books, 1997).

Martini Diaries (fiction, under the name of Leslie Ann Nash), (San Francisco, CA: Chronicle Books, 1997).

Harvard and the Unabomber: The Education of an American Terrorist, (New York: Norton, 2003).

There is sorrow enough in the natural way
From men and women to fill our day;
And when we are certain of sorrow in store,
Why do we always arrange for more?
Brothers and sisters, I bid you beware
Of giving your heart to a dog to tear.

—Rudyard Kipling

Land of Heart's Desire,
Where beauty has no ebb, decay no flood,
But joy is wisdom, time an endless song.

—W. B. Yeats

Contents

Preface   xi

Acknowledgments   xiii

Prologue: A Ghost Story   1

1. The Misunderstanding   7

2. The Summer of 1972   13

3. The Earth Life   27

4. Phineas   33

5. The Dogs of Devon   39

6. Growing up Small   51

7. The Soul of a Dog   59

8. Hamilton Farm   65

9. Special Dogs   77

10. Living at the Edge   83

11. Show Dogs   89

12. Leaving Millegan   99

13. Paradise   105

14. America Discovers Jack Russells   115

15. Searching for "Genetic Immortality"   123

16. Ifrit's Spirit   129

17. Ifrit Passes   135

18. Daisy and Bungee   139

19. Ranching the View   147

20. The Stealth and "A" Teams   153

21. Bungee's Summer   161

22. Bungee's Winter   173

23. Cricket   179

24. A Sporting Dog   193

25. Ghosts   199

26. Eternity   205

27. Millegan Return   211

Epilogue: The Future of Dogs   219

Image Information and Credits   237

Preface

The fabric of every life is woven from many threads. *We Give our Hearts to Dogs to Tear* follows two such strands in the lives of my wife Diana and myself. It's a story of our thirty years with Jack Russell terriers and a meditation on the nature of time and eternity. Thus while it is a memoir, it's not a full account of our lives. To be sure, it follows other strands as well, but only briefly and incompletely—including the controversies that engulfed us as educators and writers, our decision to abandon our teaching careers, adventures during the summer environmental educational program, financial difficulties, and, most importantly, the lives of our sons during the few brief years between our move to Montana and their departure for college. But these are described only insofar as they fit into the story and meditation that are the focus of the book.

Perhaps these other strands would be worth developing at greater length and putting into a book someday; but then again, perhaps not. This book, after all, began life as a memoir about my career as scholar and writer, but the theme had to be abandoned when it became apparent it was too boring.

There is, however, a third thread that must be followed. It concerns a few dear friends who share our love for Jack Russells and without whose encouragement the book would never have been written, much less published. For, the very multiplicity of possible threads of the book nearly did it in; and only their support rescued it.

Twenty-one trade book editors rejected the manuscript, some because they believed it had too many strands, others because it had too few. Some wanted more about our children, or our leaving teaching, or the summer program, others wanted less. Some wanted more about our dogs; most advised eliminating mention of many of them entirely. Several didn't like the criticism of purebred breeding. And all were scared to death of the subject of, well, death.

Rather, most seemed to want a trite genre book that made people laugh and didn't unduly tax minds. One death of a dog, they said, was okay, but definitely not more. And to make death the book's theme was beyond the pale. They seemed unaware that everyone who's ever owned and loved a dog has experienced its death, and those who've owned dogs their entire lives have experienced such grief repeatedly.

I wrote *We Give Our Hearts to Dogs to Tear* for them. But after many rejections I would have begun to lose confidence in the book if it had not been for the love, inspiration, and support of our very special friends Terri Zagrodnick, David and Avril Howe, and Claudette Barker, with whom we share an abiding love for Jack Russells and whose resolute faith in the book never flagged.

There are many others to whom I'm indebted as well. Steve and Libby Bodio's early admonition "not to change a word" steeled my resolve to reject bad editorial advice. Ned Shapiro, proprietor of the Pine Creek Cafe in Paradise Valley, gave me the opportunity to hone the text by reading it aloud to the patrons of his restaurant. Writers William Hjortsberg and Tim Cahill made constructive editorial comments; and by their understanding of the book belied the criticisms of those editors whose rejection of the manuscript revealed they clearly hadn't understood it. Patrick Burns, author of *American Working Terriers* provided invaluable help with fact checking and the search for historical sources. Through her long experience with Jack Russells and her concern, which I share, for the little terrier's future, Ailsa Crawford, founder of the Jack Russell Terrier Club of America, has contributed important historical insights and done much to make others aware of this book. Thanks to her careful reading of, and faith in, the manuscript (not to mention her love of dogs), my agent, Wendy Weil, provided help and insight in too many ways to mention.

Most important, I want to thank our sons David and Sidney for so patiently enduring the bad luck of having inherited two immature parents whose love of dogs is, of course, completely irrational.

And what of my wife, Diana? This story is as much hers as mine. After sharing forty-four years together, where should thanks begin, or end? Suffice to say this story could not have been lived or written without her—without her love of dogs and other animals, her willingness to take risks, her empathy for nature, her love of letters, and her encouragement to write. How many wives would have tolerated, much less urged, their husband to quit his job and move, with her, to a leaky, one-room wilderness cabin, to share it with dogs, cats, wildcats, and a coyote?

She must have been crazy, thank goodness.

Acknowledgments

The author wishes to acknowledge the sources and permissions sought for poems and photographs reproduced in this book, and to apologize to any copyright holders who could not be traced or who have been inadvertently overlooked.

The following poems appear in the text:

"Man and Dog," by Siegfried Sassoon, Copyright Siegfried Sassoon by kind permission of the Estate of George Sassoon, for non-exclusive world rights.

"Man and Dog," from SEQUENCES by Siegfried Sassoon, (c) 1957 by the Viking Press. Used with the permission of Viking Penguin, a division of Penguin Group (USA) Inc, for non-exclusive rights, US and Canada

"For a Good Dog," by Ogden Nash, (c) 1949 by Ogden Nash, reprinted by permission of Curtis Brown, Ltd.

"A Shakespearean Sonnet for Ted," by Olwen Way, quoted from *The Poetry of Dogs*, (c) 2000, by Olwen Way and reprinted with permission of the publisher, J. A. Allen, London.

Prologue

A Ghost Story

Ifrit stood at the edge of the narrow ledge above our heads, leaning over to get a better view of the 1,000-foot vertical drop beneath her. She wasn't frightened, but we were. Why had we taken this fuzzy, fourteen pound Jack Russell terrier on a mountain climbing expedition anyway? We were young and didn't anticipate the risks.

For a year we'd planned this trip with friends to climb Mount Dewey, a 11,265 foot peak in Montana's Beartooth Wilderness. And Ifrit insisted on going along. Fearless and athletic despite her small size, she'd gamely go anywhere. So here we were, scaling the rock face, passing Ifrit up over our heads to the next higher ledge, each one narrower than the other until we'd gotten stuck. Only then, when there seemed no way either up or down did we realize she could fall to her death.

"Ifrit" was the name of a mischievous genie in *Arabian Nights* who would appear suddenly and cast a spell on someone, then quickly vanish. Just so, Ifrit had entered our lives as if by magic, changed us forever, then disappeared.

But Ifrit didn't die on the mountain that day. We eventually found our way up through a rock chimney to the summit; and after enjoying the view, glissaded down a steep ice field off the peak—I sliding on my bottom with Ifrit in my arms—to the silvery lake below.

We would share many more adventures before Ifrit left us. And when her death finally came, I knew she'd been the greatest gift of my life. I could never expect such good fortune again.

Yet, as if by miracle, almost exactly a year after Ifrit departed, Bungee arrived. Long-haired and mostly white, he seemed her reincarnation. A joyous dog with a happy skip in his step, he lit up my life once again. But too soon he departed as mysteriously as he had come.

Between them, Ifrit and Bungee and their mates and pups had been my companions for thirty years as we explored the rivers, fields, and moun-

1

Ifrit Summits Mount Dewey
"She'd gamely go anywhere."

"Ifrit didn't die on the mountain that day . . . We would share many more adventures before she left us."

tains of Montana together. After they departed, their images continue to course through memory. I see us walking through a meadow of high grass or climbing a mountain or entering a dark forest. And always in the background stands the land—a silent presence that gradually envelops us until we blend into it and disappear.

* * * * *

In his poem, "The Power of the Dog," Rudyard Kipling asks, "Why in Heaven (before we are there) should we give our hearts to a dog to tear?"

"There is sorrow enough in the natural way," he writes:

> From men and women to fill our day;
> And when we are certain of sorrow in store,
> Why do we always arrange for more?
> *Brothers and sisters, I bid you beware*
> *Of giving your heart to a dog to tear . . .*
>
> When the body that lived at your single will,
> With its whimper of welcome, is stilled (how still!)
> When the spirit that answered your every mood
> Is gone—wherever it goes—for good,
> *You will discover how much you care,*
> *And will give your heart to a dog to tear.*

How should we answer Kipling? Why did I take Ifrit and Bungee into my heart, knowing someday they'd die, leaving me bereft? Why do dogs have such power over us?

Their ghosts know the answer.

* * * * *

Today I'm an old man, haunted by the ghosts of dogs and the land. They come in dreams, or sometimes when I'm lying on the couch, or driving to town for errands, or when I'm walking with my living dogs in the woods. But these visitations are not disturbing. They are the spirits of dogs and places I loved. I talk to them and they to me. We say how much we miss each other. And although before I encounter them I often feel down, after we meet I am restored.

Several of my friends, too, are haunted by the spirits of dogs. They tell me about the most special dog in their lives, now dead, who returns to give them an important message, then disappears. And I believe them.

Lands we once knew and loved return as apparitions too. They were once communities of living things that were born and eventually died. But the spirits of these lands do not die. They become ghosts.

Ghosts live beyond time. They are immortal.

Not only do dogs and land become ghosts, they become inseparable ghosts, like Siamese twins. They are spirits of dogs-in-the-land. For dogs evolved on the land. The two cannot be pulled apart simply because one dies.

The spirit of the land binds us to dogs, too. For thousands of years our mutual ancestors lived and worked the land together. And at some point during this distant past, the land became a catalyst that fused their spirits. Then people knew why they give their hearts to dogs: While dogs' bodies may not live long, it is their spirits we love and they never die.

This is a tale of such spirits. It's about the Jack Russell terriers with whom we shared the land, how each day they gave us a new reason to love them, and why their memory still haunts.

You could call it a ghost story.

1

The Misunderstanding

My salad days,
When I was green in Judgement

—William Shakespeare,
Anthony and Cleopatra

"Oh, Jack Russell terriers," Diana said. "I'd love a puppy, Georgie. If you hear one's available, please let me know."

At least, that's what I thought she said as I listened from the kitchen. How was I to know it was all a big mistake—a misunderstanding that would change our lives forever?

We were gathered, that August of 1977, at our ranch in Montana's Little Belt Mountains, an area known as Millegan Country. My wife, Diana, and I ran a wilderness program for young people there, and that summer two of Diana's cousins, Tommy and Meg Ashforth, both teenagers, had attended. Now the session was over and the children's sister, Kate, and their parents, Henry and Georgie, had come to stay for a few days then take them home.

Early that morning, Henry, Tommy, and I accompanied by our Mastiff, Una, had scrambled down the precipitous "suicide trail" into the Smith River canyon to cast flies at large trout lying in deep green pools under the red and orange limestone cliffs. Georgie, Kate, and Meg joined Diana on a horseback ride to the open high country known as Gaddis Hill.

And in the evening, our excursions done, we assembled for dinner in the kitchen house—the one-room log cabin that served as combination kitchen, dining, and living room. Sore in the legs and fanny, we ate well and shared recollections of the day. It was then, with the meal over, as I stood at the kitchen sink washing dishes, that I thought I heard Diana say she wanted a Jack Russell.

7

I'd never heard of the terrier before and couldn't tell a Jack Russell from Charley Russell. But that didn't matter. What did—or seemed to—was that Diana liked the dog and her birthday was coming up in a month. A puppy would make the ideal gift.

Except that we didn't need another dog. We already had two cats, two wildcats, a coyote, eleven horses—and our beloved Mastiff, Una. And we were broke. Friends and relatives whispered about our irresponsible lifestyle. They thought us crazy to live in the Montana wilderness with just animals as friends. Adding another mouth to feed would only convince them we were beyond help. And perhaps we were.

But being called irresponsible never stopped us before. When it came to animals neither of us knew the meaning of "enough."

Throughout our married life we'd indulged each other's weakness for pets. When we were married we'd taken our two Great Danes, Lufra and Isola, and an ocelot, Hobbididence, with us on the honeymoon. After they died, we replaced them with two Irish Wolfhounds, Ravelin and Williwolf. In between there were hampsters, a guinea pig, various coyotes, sparrow- and red-tailed hawks, six pheasants, a dozen quail, a love bird, a Puli, several horses, a mule, and around thirty cats.

In truth, we craved the company of animals. We couldn't have too many. They were our psychic capital, providing a reservoir of emotional support against a growing sense of desperation. But desperation is the mother of initiative; and without it, we wouldn't even have been there.

* * * * *

Like many Montanans, Diana and I were refugees. In the early 1970s we had been teachers in Minnesota—I a professor of philosophy at Macalester College in Saint Paul and she an instructor in environmental studies at the Minneapolis public schools. Our three sons, David, Lawrance, and Sidney attended a fine St. Paul school. But I wasn't happy. I had become a philosopher to pursue the life of reflection. But those weren't reflective times. Protests over the war in Vietnam had ripped the campus apart, transforming students and faculty alike into activists and severing our last links with Plato and Spinoza. By 1972 I began to look for an exit.

Perhaps, I told Diana, we could find a small place in Montana to spend summers in quiet contemplation and recharge our batteries. So, during the school and college spring break that year, David (then a high school sophomore) and I drove to Montana to look for land. But every parcel was either too expensive or insufficiently remote.

But David wouldn't let me be discouraged. "We'll know the right place when we find it," he said. "We'll just say, 'This is it.'"

With two days remaining of our vacation before returning to St. Paul we visited a real estate agent named Corky Salo in the tiny town of Cascade. Did he have anything to show us? we asked.

"Might," he replied. "There's a place up in Millegan that could come on the market, but I'm not sure you can get there yet. Too much snow."

A virtually roadless mountainous region of national forest and private ranches along the spectacular Smith River canyon between the Big and Little Belt Mountains, Millegan was remote in any season and inaccessible in winter. But Salo's assistant, Warren Hastings agreed to try to take us.

"I'm bringing three shovels," he warned, "Cuz there'll be lots of snow." From Cascade we climbed bare hills that looked down on the Missouri plain, over a mountain pass called Millegan Hill, then past rolling slopes where pine forests framed snow-covered meadows. We plowed and shoveled our way through deep drifts until we came to collapsing log buildings hidden in a declivity next to a spring.

We peered into a hole in the roof of the log barn and through the glassless windows of the bunkhouse and blacksmith's shed.

"It's called the Ben Dunn place," Hastings explained. Then he drove us across an open field that seemed to go forever, and suddenly braked hard. Getting out, we stood in awe at the lip of the magnificent canyon—a place we would come to call, "The Point." In the distance, the Little Belt Mountains crowded the sky. A thousand feet below, the Smith River meandered through snow-covered meadows. A prairie falcon circled overhead. We stood in awe.

"This is it," David said.

* * * * *

Fifty-five miles from the nearest town, ten from the closest neighbor, and thirty-five miles from the nearest maintained road, the Ben Dunn place had neither telephone nor electricity. Its drinking water came from a pipe in the ground that poured its contents into a sunken oak barrel. The only buildings were dilapidated log structures—the barn, blacksmith's shed, bunkhouse whose windows had never known glass, a granary with a roofless outhouse attached, and the original, packrat-infested homesteader's cabin, its log exterior covered with plywood siding on the outside and beaverboard on the inside.

Comprising 3,000 acres, the Ben Dunn place was far more than we could afford or manage. It was too expensive, too primitive, and too

"A thousand feet below, the Smith River meandered through snow-covered meadows."

"'This is it,' David said."

remote. The annual payments exceeded two-thirds of my before-tax income. Although the seller, Frank Murphy, agreed to lease pasturage from us for 80 cows and calves, that would generate just $4,000 annually and required watering, rotating, and salting the cattle while maintaining twenty miles of fence lines.

"You can't possibly afford it," Alexander Blewett, our Great Falls attorney said. A white-haired, fatherly man, he knew irresponsibility when he saw it. Fixing a kindly gaze on us he added for emphasis, "I strongly advise against purchase."

Given such encouragement, how could we not plunge ahead? Seduced by the land, we bought it, resolving to think about payments later. We signed the contract and left Blewett's office giddy with excitement.

It was not until the cold light of the following morning that Diana and I looked at each other and asked. "What've we done?"

2

The Summer of 1972

*In the highlands you woke up in the
morning and thought:
Here I am, where I ought to be.*

—Isak Dinesen,
Out of Africa

Diana and I watched David, Lawrance, and Sidney set up the umbrella tent in a field of dandelions by the blacksmith's shed.

"The boys can stay in the tent and the cats in the bunkhouse," she said. "But where do we and Ravelin sleep?"

I pointed to the cabin behind us. Twelve feet square, it didn't look inviting. Sheets of its rusty corrugated roof were missing. A mountain bluebird, apparently having taken up residence there, flew out of a hole of the unpainted plywood siding. As we opened the door, a packrat—another resident—scurried across the floor. A propane heater stood in one corner; a propane stove, refrigerator, and sink that emptied its contents into a bucket in the other; and a double bed in the third.

"It's grand," Diana said. "We'll call it 'the Manse.'"

Below the Manse, water poured from the rusty pipe into the barrel. Opposite it stood the bunkhouse we would call "the Cat House"; to our right, the blacksmith's shed and beyond it, the log corral, granary, and barn. Sheets of the barn's steel roof, like the Manse's, were missing.

In short, there was nothing of value here, but everything the heart could desire.

As we explored around the buildings we felt like kids in a candy store. That morning we'd arrived from St. Paul in the family station wagon along with assorted camping gear and Ravelin, our Irish Wolfhound, Burr the Siamese cat, Thunderfoot the Abyssinian, and our two wild cats—Zoomie

"'It's grand,' Diana said. 'We'll call it The Manse.'"

the Margay and Mumtazi the Indian Fishing cat. It would be our first Millegan summer, a time that would remain shimmering in memory.

* * * * *

We found a retired carpenter in Cascade, Montana named Charley Reissing willing to come and help us build a cabin. A slim, white-haired and cheerful man about sixty-five, Charley stayed a month, sleeping by the barn in his own tent and taking his meals with us. Together, he and our family, armed with nail-pullers and crowbars, tore down the blacksmith's shed and built the log cabin for cooking and eating we would soon dub "the Kitchen House." Diana, Ravelin, and I slept in the Manse and the boys moved into the bunkhouse with Burr, Thunderfoot, Mumtazi, and Zoomie. In evenings, as coyotes howled outside we sat on the Kitchen House deck and listened to Charley tell stories about Charles M. Russell, the famous western artist he had known as a boy.

When not carpentering we explored the land. We hiked to the river, where the boys tied a rope from a tree, swinging from it into the deep emerald pool below. We descended into the mysterious Black canyon, discovering ancient aboriginal paintings in a cave there. We fly-fished, catching and releasing the big brown and rainbow trout. Together with Ravelin, I blazed a near-vertical trail out of the canyon, from the river to the Point—a feat that at places required lifting Ravelin's 150 pound frame onto my shoulder and heaving him up from ledge to ledge. Our boys called the route, "Suicide Trail."

But we soon discovered this wasn't just land. Millegan had its own history, and we became part of it.

* * * * *

One morning a brown pickup truck stopped at the Manse. A stocky, red-faced man wearing a battered Stetson got out, an unfiltered cigarette dangling from his lips. His small blue eyes twinkled as he said, "I'm Frank Murphy and I sold you this place. Now, let me show you what you bought."

I hopped into his truck and off we went, up a narrow trail that switched through the pines to the top of Gaddis, where we peered into the darkness of the Black Canyon on the other side. Along the way, he described the local history and pointed out fences, springs, and boundaries.

"Your property is named the Ben Dunn place," Frank explained, "after the first white owner who moved here in 1916." But Blackfoot Indians came before Dunn. Teepee rings signifying their occupation

"In short, there was nothing of value here, but everything
the heart could desire."

were visible in the pasture, and the steep trail they built—known as "the Packdown"—was still the best way to the river. In the 1920s, Millegan was bootlegging country, where cowboys made whisky in high country caves beyond the reach of federal agents.

Ten miles south of Gaddis, Frank continued, lay what had once been the town of Lingshire. Seventy years earlier it was a thriving homesteader community, with a school and dances every Saturday night. Then Wellington Rankin, a successful trial lawyer with political connections and an insatiable hankering for land, bought everybody out and hired ex-convicts as ranch hands. By the 1930s, when Frank was a small boy, Lingshire had a reputation as a tough place and he was afraid to go there. So were many others and the town died.

A bootlegger's widow appropriately named Bessie Vineyard went to work for Dunn, and eventually bought the place from him. She was a tough cowgal who could shoe a horse better than any man could, and in 1948 she married her neighbor, Jerauld Cope. Bessie and Jerauld lived at the Ben Dunn place until, as all Milleganers eventually discover, this uncompromising country became too hard for them. They sold the ranch to Frank and moved to Townsend, Montana. Now he'd sold it to us and already wished he hadn't.

He stopped the truck where the road descends steeply eastward through the forest to the river. We contemplated the Smith as it meandered 2,000 feet below.

"God, how I love this land," he said.

* * * * *

In Millegan country, we learned, a "neighbor" was anyone within thirty miles. And as this comprised fewer than twenty people, it wasn't long before we became friends with all.

Occasionally I visited Lingshire to fish Rock Creek. Although Rankin died a few years earlier and much of his land was sold to pay inheritance taxes, his Lingshire property still encompassed the entire derelict town. There we met "Pap," Rankin's foreman. With full beard and broad chest, he looked like Gabby Hayes, the actor who played character parts in many westerns in the '40s and '50s. Pap loved Rankin, perhaps because he had sprung Pap from the penitentiary. He marveled at the ranch as it used to be, when it was the biggest in Montana. "One of his spreads," Pap told me, "covered 500 square miles and had only one cross fence running down the middle of it. You could ride days and never need open a gate. It was special."

"We soon discovered this wasn't just land. Millegan had its wn history, and we became part of it."

Thirty miles north over the Millegan Hill pass, on the Smith River tributary known as Hound Creek lay the Carlile Ranch, run by Jim and Marie Carlile and their two sons, Jeff and Jerome. Jim's father, a descendent of Civil War general Philip Sheridan and a close friend of the artist, Charles Russell, homesteaded the ranch in 1884 and ran it until his death in 1917. For many years the family also operated a coal mine on the property, but eventually sold it to concentrate on their livestock operation. As theirs wasn't a large ranch, however, Jim and his family supplemented their incomes with contract trucking, combining, and haying.

The Carliles always worked hard for a living, but their generosity never flagged. We depended on them in many ways. The pavement ended at their ranch and so did the telephone line. Often, on our way to Great Falls we stopped there for coffee and, occasionally, to use the phone in their barn.

Ten miles north of our place lay Millegan. Like Lingshire, it had been a thriving community, but now only an empty schoolhouse, four ranches, and a row of mail boxes remained. Three times a week I drove there to pick up mail, where I'd stop to discuss the weather with Carl and Betty Anderson and their son and daughter-in-law, Richard and Debbie. Carl, who had homesteaded around Millegan since the First World War, loved a good joke. He glued a nickel to the floor of the kitchen, and collapsed with laughter every time someone tried to pick it up.

A few days after we arrived, Ted Cope came to visit. Jerauld and Bessie's nephew, Ted, was the last of that once-large clan that settled along the Smith after World War I. We'd heard about Ted from Warren Hastings who told us, "You'll find Ted different." When I asked how different, he replied, "He's mountain people, and mountain people are just, well, different."

And we soon learned what Hastings meant: Ted and all Milleganers ignored time. They never rushed. They lived in the moment, savoring especially the company of others. Once they came to visit, it seemed they'd never leave.

"Want a beer?" I asked Ted as he got out of his pickup.

"No thanks," he replied, as he flicked his cigarette ashes into the rolled cuff of his Levis. "Can't stay. Just came to say hello." Two hours later we were still standing in the same spot, "saying hello"—by which time Ted's cuffs were stuffed with the residue paper of cigarettes he'd carefully field-stripped after smoking.

"Bud Dawson come by yet?" Ted asked as he finally made a move to leave.

"No," I replied. "Who's he?"

"You'll find out," Ted said, smiling like the Cheshire cat.

* * * * *

Right on cue the next morning a red stock truck pulled up to the Kitchen House carrying two big brown geldings already saddled. Two small, thin people got out, each holding a cigarette in one hand and a can of beer in the other. Like so many in Millegan they seemed to be in their mid-sixties.

"I'm Bud Dawson," the man said, "and this is my wife, Annie Laurie." Bud wore a new Stetson and a big silver belt buckle and looked like an aging Gary Cooper, hard and lean. Annie Laurie seemed nervous, anorexic, and unsteady on her feet.

"I own the Tenderfoot," Bud explained, referring to the land on the crystalline Smith River tributary opposite us, "and keep cattle there each summer. Jerauld gave me a right to take them through your place, down the Packdown. So don't try to stop me. And don't you try trespassing on my place, neither. Jack Ramsey, who sold me the Tenderfoot told me I owned both sides of the river. And just so we understand each other, we let nobody on our place. Nobody."

"Want a beer?" I asked.

"Don't mind if I do," he replied, "now that we understand each other."

They stayed for three hours and four beers. Bud, we learned, enjoyed a reputation for cantankerous territoriality. He relished patrolling his land on horseback wearing a six-shooter and threatening to punch holes in the canoe or rubber raft of any fisherman or floater who dared set foot on his land.

And he was always looking for more land.

"I don't want much land," he said as he finished his last beer, "I just want what borders me."

As we bordered him this did not reassure, so I changed the subject. "Know where we might find a couple of good horses?" I asked.

"Don't tell me you dudes can ride," Bud replied sarcastically. "But if you promise never to ride them on my place I'll tell you. See Art Watson. He lives in Benton Gulch."

* * * * *

The road to Watson's took us south past Lingshire, through a swampy meadow called Beaver Flat, then westward, into a lush green valley known as Benton Gulch surrounded by tall, forested hills. Watson's cabins and corral sat at the foot of the hills, about two miles from the road.

Art greeted us with a big smile. Eighty-one years old, gray, and balding, he nevertheless looked as healthy as a horse. And would he sell Diana one? That depended, he said, on whether she could ride—really ride—because his didn't like to poke along.

"Let's go the corral," he said. "I'll put my mother's old saddle on Dandy. He's nine and fitted with afterburners. And Diana, if you can stay on him you can have the horse and the saddle too, for a fair price."

His father, Art explained, emigrated from Scotland as a small boy with his parents and two brothers. He fought for the Union during the Civil War, was wounded and honorably discharged, and in 1864 came to Montana to seek his fortune. In 1870 he joined the gold rush to Diamond City, which was just down the road from where Art now lived. Diamond City lay in a narrow valley called Confederate Gulch, beside a small stream just over the hill from Benton Gulch. It was the site of one of the richest gold strikes in the west, and in the 1860s boasted "the longest main street in the world"—a dusty road lined with ramshackle buildings that snaked through the gulch for perhaps fifteen miles.

Art's father struck gold himself in Benton Gulch and mined it until it played out. Then he rode to California, drove 3,000 sheep back home, and began ranching. After establishing himself, his father rode to Fort Benton, boarded a steamer to St. Louis, then a train to New York, where he found and married a Connecticut girl and brought her back to the ranch. They had eight children—three girls and five boys—and hired a tutor to stay at the ranch and teach them. But the kids' real schoolroom was the saddle.

Art and his ranch had cast a spell and we found it hard to leave. But at dark we did, and the next day Art delivered the horse and saddle. Dandy would be the best riding horse we ever had and remained with us until he died, eighteen years later. Also coming with the purchase, as a bonus, was Art's lasting friendship.

* * * *

One July morning a small man walked by the Kitchen House and did not stop until we hailed him. About five feet tall, he wore rubber hip boots folded down to his knees and a tattered army fatigue jacket. His name was Scott Allen.

"I live down on the Smith," he explained. "You seen my cabin by the Packdown? I got a shepherd's wagon downstream from there, too, run a trapline up the Tenderfoot and have 'nother wagon up by the falls."

"Stop for a bite?" I asked.

"Naw," Allen replied. I'm goin' to the top of Gaddis to pick rhubarb."

"A five mile trip, just for rhubarb?" I asked.

"Good with griddlecakes," he replied.

"I was born in Sam Houston, Texas," he later told our Millegan neighbor Vernie Kitson, who recorded his story, "and raised in the Oklahoma territory by two bachelors. I think they was outlaws." But he wasn't certain exactly who they were or when he was born. Around 1912 he and a friend started a business rounding up wild horses in Oklahoma and driving them to Michigan to sell. After working as a lumberjack for a while, he joined the Army in 1915, and served on the Mexican border. When World War I broke out two years later, he was sent to France, where he was gassed. In 1924 he was mustered out of the army, moved to Millegan and became a trapper. In 1942 he rejoined the army, fought in the Pacific and stayed in uniform for twenty years. In 1962 he returned to Millegan and resumed trapping, which he's been doing ever since. His woman, whom he called his "squaw," was in a nursing home, but Scott still lived in his grass-roofed log cabin by the river. And what he did was walk vast distances every day. "But I can't do forty miles a day anymore," he confessed.

Our children would visit Scott's eight-foot square cabin often. He cooked them griddle cakes on a wood stove made from a fifty-gallon oil drum, and told them stories about growing up in Oklahoma territory, fighting bears, trapping beaver, and meeting mountain lions.

* * * * *

And so went the summer: bright days and long hikes and rides over broad, open country and deep forests. A summer of mornings hammering nails with Reissing and afternoons repairing fences, carrying salt, and driving cattle. Of treks down Suicide Trail with Ravelin and the boys; of swimming in the river and stalking trout; of visits with Pap and Scott Allen, and rides up the Tenderfoot and over Gaddis Hill; of drinking coffee on mail days with Carl and Betty Anderson; of drives to Great Falls for supplies, punctuated by stopovers with Jim, Jerome, and Marie Carlile; of trading barbs about boundaries with Bud and Annie Laurie over beer; of visits from Art Watson and Jerauld and Bessie Cope who sat on the Kitchen House steps and talked about Millegan's past. And of walking, every evening, rain or shine, to the Point, to stand in silence.

"One July morning a small man walked by the Kitchen House and did not stop until we hailed him . . . His name was Scott Allen."

"Our children visited Scott's cabin regularly. He cooked them griddle cakes on a wood stove made from a fifty-gallon oil drum, and told them stories about growing up in Oklahoma territory, fighting bears."

We had fallen in love with Millegan. Like a *femme fatale* who draws her lover into a life of recklessness, it had seduced us. But when in September we returned to Minnesota for the new school year, it was as though we had wakened from a dream. If our summer idyll had made our cares disappear, its ending brought them back with a vengeance.

I was thrown back into the campus wars. And just when I thought things couldn't get worse, they did. At dark during rush hour, a neighbor's son had gone into the yard of our St. Paul home to retrieve a ball and forgot to close the gate behind him. Ravelin got out and was immediately killed by a car. Our quiet, gentle, and closest friend, hiking buddy and constant companion with whom I'd blazed Suicide Trail, was gone. How I wished at least he'd died in Millegan where his soul belonged, but the ranch at that moment seemed far away.

Even though Diana found a teaching job that fall we were still broke. And the first year's ranch mortgage payment was coming due.

"We've got to think of something," I said.

"Maybe start a summer camp?" Diana suggested.

Just so, one desperate act led to another.

3

The Earth Life

That was the life I desired—the life the heart can conceive
—the earth life.

—W.H. Hudson,
Far Away and Long Ago, *1918*

When grasping a tiger by the tail, we reasoned, one best use two hands. Having bought a ranch too big to manage with money we didn't have, the next year we rolled the dice—double or nothing—and started a summer environmental and wilderness program for teenagers, calling it, Chase Ranch for Young People. Our sons joined the staff.

In May I returned to the ranch and with Charley Reissing, tapped a spring up the canyon, buried a half mile of pipe, and brought running water to the buildings. We built a bathhouse containing sinks, showers, and flush toilets. Diana and the boys joined us in June.

The first campers arrived in July, staying in wood-floored army squad tents Charley and I had set up. We offered fishing, riding, backpacking, and, for the older boys and girls, rock climbing. We taught fly tying and ecology. University life science professors and state game experts visited periodically to conduct classes in zoology, botany, geology, and limnology. Two years later, Charley and I put up a third building containing space for campers to tie flies, work leather, read, and play games. We called it the "Hobby House."

A new dog joined us. Two months after Ravelin died, Una, an eight-week old Mastiff, entered our lives. Quiet and gentle like Ravelin, she had a wry sense of humor and never missed an opportunity to play. She became the ranch jester and the campers adored her. She had an endless imagination for making up games, whether it was hide and seek with coyotes, chasing (but never catching) gophers, or foolishly challenging porcupines. Her favorite pastime was to stick her head in an empty bucket and yelp at the top of her lungs. The acoustics inside the bucket produced an echo she found addictive.

Our lives had shifted to fast forward and continued accelerating. Each June we fled the political chaos of Macalester to face the frantic stress and fun of the summer program; then in September we closed the buildings and dashed back to face another Minnesota winter of discontent. But the pace became too much. By 1975 I had burned out.

Running into a colleague on the stairs of Old Main, I said, "This is no place for philosophy. I'm moving to Montana."

"Lot's of philosophy there," he replied.

* * * * *

So in the winter of 1975, with David in college, Lawrance headed there, and Sidney (having received a scholarship) on his way to boarding school, Diana and I—pushed by desperation and pulled by the allure of Millegan—quit our jobs, sold our St. Paul house along with my Steinway piano and her Queen Anne desk, and moved to the Ben Dunn place vowing to stay forever.

With neither job nor savings and with the summer program barely breaking even, I would embark on a new career as a writer—not realizing that, according to the Author's Guild, just a few hundred individuals in the entire country made a living from writing alone. But being at the ranch far removed from the world of money, jobs, and campus politics we found it impossible to worry.

And as it turned out we were right not to. For we'd escaped, not from reality, but to it.

* * * * *

We settled into the Manse and the seasons defined our days.

When the campers left and fall arrived, the land was ours alone. Each morning after breakfast, I walked to the Hobby House to write. In afternoons, Diana and I hiked or rode into the dark shadows of the Smith River canyon, frequently startling a deer grazing in the flood plain or bear hungrily devouring chokecherries. Occasionally I descended Suicide Trail with Una to the Smith, to stalk spawning brown trout until my fingers turned numb and ice formed on the rod's guides. In evenings, we sat in the Kitchen House and read by the light of kerosene and Coleman lanterns. Once a month we drove to Great Falls for supplies or to make phone calls from a pay phone at the airport.

Galvanized by the shortening days we drove into the forest with Una to fell and buck trees and cut and split logs for the wood stove. We turned the horses loose to winter on Gaddis Hill where blowing wind kept grass clear of snow.

In winter our isolation was complete. The Millegan Road filled with snowdrifts fifteen feet high and would not see a plow for six months. Although occasionally, Debbie Anderson's mother Jackie Bush or Richard Anderson dropped by on snowmobile to check on us, often weeks passed without our seeing another human soul. After dinner we sat on the Salvation Army sofa by the wood stove, with Una at our feet, Mumtazi in my lap, Burr in Diana's, and Thunderfoot between us and watched as elk, their breath visible in the dry frigid air, careened down the hill, a herd without thunder, sending up clouds of snow carried by the wind.

Occasionally we snow-shoed to the top of Gaddis to check on the horses, knowing that at any moment temperatures could drop to forty below and a raging blizzard appear from nowhere. Driving to Millegan to pick up mail—when possible at all—usually required putting forty-pound tire chains on all four wheels of the pickup, then digging through snowdrifts that blocked the road. Even so, we sometimes found ourselves high-centered alone in the dark with snow up to the truck windshield and no one to call for help.

In spring we greeted the mountain bluebirds that arrived without fail on the vernal equinox to build nests in the eaves of the Kitchen House and Manse. When warm days coaxed the gophers from hibernation, we watched bobcats catch and collect them to feed their young. We brought the horses down from Gaddis. We checked and repaired twenty miles of fencing on near-vertical slopes, through forests, up canyons and down to the river and back. We watched herds of antelope canter across the range like wildebeest on the Serengeti. Occasionally we ventured into the canyon to renew our acquaintance with the river and watch deer and bear graze the first lush grasses of the flood plain.

In summer, we greeted the returning campers and resumed the summer program. We led backpacking and mountain climbing expeditions to Glacier and Yellowstone National parks and into the Beartooth, Absaroka, Crazy, and Big and Little Belt Mountains.

Throughout the seasons we enjoyed the riches of solitude, as at the end of each day, every season, we walked to the Point with Una and the cats to meditate on the view. We felt like privileged visitors as we enjoyed the company of wild animals—mountain lions, lynx, bobcats, elk, whitetail and mule deer, antelope, big horn sheep, mountain goats, porcupines, skunks, coyotes, black bears, badgers, hawks, and falcons—who called Millegan home and who always seemed surprised to find us among them.

* * * * *

I wrote prolifically, but sold nothing. Rejection slips mounted and savings dwindled. I began looking for a job but without success. We were broke.

Poverty increased our isolation. We couldn't afford airfare to visit our children at school or college, or fly them home for holidays. Alone in the wilderness, we forged tight bonds with our animals. Having no television, we watched Zoomie, the Margay from Mexico, instead. Suffering from attention deficit disorder, he readily succumbed to cabin fever and sought relief by running around the kitchen house at warp speed, banking off the walls and thereby rearranging pictures and clearing shelves of books.

Gentle Mumtazi was my constant reading companion. Each evening this orphaned "fishing cat" from India whom we adopted, would plant her furry forty-pound body in my lap, suck at my shirt as though it were a teat, and purr herself to sleep.

When just a kitten she had nearly died of distemper; and as she was a wildcat veterinarians refused to treat her. So I had nursed her back to health myself, injecting fluids into her body every three hours for a month until her body threw off the disease. And ever since, she treated me as her mother. Like her web-footed cousins in her native India, whose habitat lies along lakes and rivers where they prey on aquatic life, Mumtazi loved to stalk geese in the ranch pond. She was equally enthusiastic about fishing. When, occasionally I brought a trout up from the river alive and dumped it into a horse trough, Mumtazi dove in after it. She was never happier than during such moments.

Sweet Burr, the chocolate-point Siamese, needed constant reassurance. The worrier of the family, he found life in this big country perpetually bewildering. By contrast, his plucky little friend, Thunderfoot the Abyssinian, charged through life with nary a self-doubt. As he considered it his duty to rid the world of mountain bluebirds, we tied two large bells around his neck—one on a foot-long thong that dragged on the ground behind him. Yet he still caught the birds.

Little Orphan Annie, our coyote, came to us as a tiny pup, brought by the official of Montana's Department of Fish, Wildlife and Parks in charge of caring for abandoned or wounded wildlife. Would we, he asked, adopt the little girl? Annie quickly fit in with our little troop. I tried to teach her to hunt by catching ground squirrels alive and giving them to her to kill. But she refused to harm them, preferring to befriend them instead. So I shot her meals for her. Each afternoon we went hunting together. I took my .22 rifle and the two of us walked into the horse pasture. Annie sat quietly at my feet as I took aim and dispatched a squirrel. After the rodent dropped, she ran up and ate it.

* * * * *

Such was our life of rustic bliss and financial terror when the Ashforths came to visit that August of 1977. We had no inkling that a little dog was about to change everything.

4

Phineas

What are the dogs that we today call . . .
Jack Russell terriers?

> —*D. Brian Plummer,*
> The Complete Jack Russell Terrier, *1980*

One sees them everywhere today;
all sorts and conditions of terriers
and all of them called "Jack Russells"

> — *"Dan Russell,"*
> Jack Russell and his Terriers, *1979*

A week after the Ashforths left I drove with Una to Great Falls for supplies, stopping at the airport to call our answering service from the pay phone.

"Mrs. Ashforth called from Connecticut," the message operator said, adding, "Something about a terrier." So I returned Georgie's call.

"I found a Jack Russell for Diana," Georgie told me. "A bitch belonging to Aurelia Bolton, an old school chum, whose female Jack Russell, Adelaide, whelped three pups six weeks ago. If Diana's interested, give her a call."

"Great," I answered enthusiastically, being too embarrassed to admit I wouldn't recognize a Jack Russell if I tripped over one. For all I knew, the dog could be larger than a Great Dane or smaller than a Chihuahua. All that mattered was that Diana wanted one and her birthday was coming up.

I immediately called the Boltons. Aurelia's husband, Perry, answered. "We have a nice little tri-color male pup," he said. "One hundred and fifty dollars. We can air ship him to you."

The price seemed right. But having gone this far I was too embarrassed to ask, "What is a Jack Russell terrier, anyway?" So I tried indirection.

33

"What's the pup look like?" I asked.

"Like any other JR," he answered.

"How big is he?" I persisted.

"Average size," he replied.

We were getting nowhere. So I took the plunge. "Well, I'd like to buy him if shipping isn't too expensive," I said. He promised to check on freight costs and told me to call back in a couple of days for the answer.

What began on impulse had quickly developed momentum of its own. Driving home, I began having second thoughts. A new puppy is a lot of work and expense, I thought. Housebreaking. Distemper shots. Wet spots on rugs. Perhaps I should ask Diana if she really wants one.

So as we were settling onto the couch that evening I asked her, "Guess what I'm giving you for your birthday?"

"What?" she answered excitedly.

"A Jack Russell terrier!" I replied, expecting her to exclaim, "Wonderful! Just what I've always wanted!"

Instead, she gave me a funny look and said, "That's nice. What're they like?"

"I thought you knew!" I answered, suppressing panic. "I positively heard you tell Georgie you wanted one."

"I did not," she replied emphatically. "All I said was I'd like to know about them."

"So am I to understand," Diana continued, absent-mindedly tugging at Una's right ear, "that you've committed us to buy a dog we know nothing about? For all we know, it could be as furry at a Komondor or bald as a Mexican hairless, as big as a Newfoundland or small as a Chihuahua. And suppose *it is a small dog*. What then?"

"Good grief," I replied. "I never thought of that."

A small dog, Diana reminded me, could never survive the rugged conditions of ranch life. Even if it didn't fall off a cliff or disappear in a snowdrift, predators would gobble it like finger food. Coyotes passed within a few feet of our cabin every morning and evening. Mountain lions and bears were abundant. Thirty-pound badgers lurked under the ground in our horse pasture, ready to tear a small dog to shreds. We hiked or rode miles each day and frequently forded the Smith, a river too deep and swift for small dogs. In winter, deep snow covered the ground. How could a pint-sized creature take a pee in that?

Besides, although we loved dogs of every size, the thought of a small one seemed, well, a bit humdrum. Diana and I had grown up with small dogs—she with toy and miniature poodles, I with Dachshunds. Small dogs were too familiar. We wanted something different. That's why since we were married we'd had only giants—Great Danes, Irish Wolfhounds, Mastiffs.

No, we decided, a small dog just wouldn't do. And that's that. So it was imperative that we find out if a Jack Russell terrier is a small dog, before it was too late.

We resolved to ask the Boltons.

* * * * *

Diana stood by my elbow as I placed the call from the airport pay phone. Perry answered. "Total shipping costs," he said, "including freight, crate, insurance, and tax come to $32.97."

"Hmmm," I replied neutrally, knowing full well that such a low fare for shipment deprived us of a good excuse for backing out of the sale. "Diana is here. She'd like to know more about the pup," I stalled. "What's his disposition like?"

"Like any Jack Russell's," he replied.

More queries got us no further. We were learning nothing about the pup. "Perhaps we should back out," Diana whispered in my ear.

But I had no exit strategy. I couldn't very well admit that we'd decided not to buy the pup because we didn't know a blessed thing about the dog. The Bolton's would think us idiots to have agreed to buy it in the first place.

Desperate for an excuse to cancel the sale, I decided to plead poverty. "That $32.97 shipping seems awfully steep," I ventured.

"My God, man," Perry cried, "We're practically giving the pup away. Do you want him or not?"

Perry had shamed us into a corner. There was no graceful way out. To save face, we had to take the pup.

"Oh, we want him," I parried, weakly. "I'll put a check in the mail."

"I'll ship him Wednesday," Perry concluded.

* * * *

So an eight-week-old pup was flying 2,500 miles from Maryland to Montana to join our family and we hadn't the foggiest idea what it was. "Perhaps Carl or Betty can tell us something about the breed," Diana suggested as we drove through Millegan on the way home.

"See the nickel's still there," I said to Carl as we entered. "Know anything about Jack Russell terriers?" I asked Betty, as she handed me a cup of steaming black coffee.

"Is it a dog?" she asked.

Diana and Phineas, Spring 1978
"Watching them I thought, 'Perhaps a Jack Russell isn't such a bad
birthday present, after all.'"

No sooner had we gotten back to the ranch than Bud and Annie Laurie Dawson showed up in their red stock truck.

"What do you know about Jack Russell terriers?" I asked Bud, as he emptied his second beer.

"What's that?" he replied, "Some kind of street gang?"

"It's a dog," I replied.

"I sure hope you're not getting another," Annie Laurie chimed. "You already got one, and as far as Bud's concerned that's too many. We'd better not catch it chasing cattle."

* * * * *

On September 20, we waited anxiously at Northwest Airlines' cargo terminal for the pup to arrive. An attendant appeared, carrying a small crate.

Inside was a little black, brown, and white face looking at us with a serious expression. He had droopy ears, black cheeks with white blaze, brown eyebrows, large dark eyes, and a funny long nose.

And he was very, very small.

Diana opened the crate and, squatting, pondered the pup. The little guy returned her gaze solemnly, without blinking.

"I'll call him Phineas," she said, "after Phineas Finn, the hero in the Anthony Trollope *Palliser* novel I'm reading. Trollope's Phineas wasn't big either, but he had good character."

Watching them I thought, "Perhaps a Jack Russell isn't such a bad birthday present, after all."

5

The Dogs of Devon

The terrier was to remain a dog small enough to enter any earth or drain large enough to hold a fox. Size was not desired . . . To go to earth, he had to be neither too heavy nor too tall . . . To win the battles under ground, he needed a strong constitution, and one able to withstand wet, cold, and fatigue. To win battles, courage was necessary, and with it the power to bear extreme punishment, without flinching or losing heart.

> —*Edward C. Ash,*
> Dogs: Their History and Development, *1927*

The Jack Russell terrier is named after Reverend John Russell, the nineteenth-century Anglican clergyman who developed the dog. Throughout his long life—he died in 1883 at age eighty-eight—Russell passionately devoted himself to foxhunting. To serve this sport he created, through careful breeding, the spunky little terrier bearing his name. So Jack Russells and foxhunting go together like peanut butter and jelly: One cannot understand the dog without knowing what he was bred to do.

Russell fell in love with foxhunting while growing up in Devon in Southwest England, a land of broad, open moors and meadows and clear rivers, not unlike our Montana. He would "ride to hounds" several times a week throughout his life. At fourteen, he was nearly expelled from school for secretly keeping a pack of nine foxhounds with a local farmer. As a scholarship student at Oxford University living on a small allowance, each weekend he rented a one-eyed horse named Charlie and joined the Duke of Beaufort's hunt across hills outside Oxford at a place called Sanford Brake.

Foxhunting required dogs: long-legged fox hounds to chase the fox and smaller terriers to go underground after the fox when it dove into its den. The terrier's job was not to kill the fox but to drive him out of his hole so the chase could continue. This was the terrier's vocation. Its name, derived from the Latin word "terra," meaning earth, signified its function. But it also symbolized the role that land played in the ancient and ubiquitous partnership between dogs and humans.

Somewhere around 12,000 years ago dogs and people began to learn the mutual advantages of cooperation. The wolf-like ancestors of modern dogs found that scavenging in villages and joining human hunts was a more reliable way to find food than killing game themselves; and the early hunter-gatherers learned it was to their advantage to take dogs as hunting partners. A few thousand years later, the advent of agriculture offered still more ways to cooperate. In exchange for food and shelter, dogs herded and guarded livestock and killed varmints that threatened crops.

As this relationship evolved, it deepened, taking on more dimensions as dogs and people found new ways to help each other. And fostering this cooperation in all its forms was the land. Just as Russell's love of riding the moors of Devon led him to foxhunting and through this to dogs, so it always was the land that brought dogs and people together. By creating the jobs dogs can do, the human activities of farming, herding, and hunting made cooperation mutually beneficial. And by working on the land together, dogs and men became companions. Apart from the land, there would have been little reason to cooperate, and without sharing it, no occasion for friendship.

Over time the land also shaped the dogs, who became more specialized. Bred by farmers, herders, and hunters from different regions with different climates for different jobs, they developed varying skills and conformation. But these ancient agriculturalists did not create "breeds" in the modern sense. They kept types of dogs, such as hounds, spaniels, and retrievers—dogs that were differentiated not by pedigrees or papers but by where they lived and what they did.

Among these types were terriers. And like other dogs at the time, when Russell was at Oxford the various terriers weren't distinct "breeds." Breeders did not adhere to a "closed stud book," which stipulated that dogs may only mate with others descended from the same foundation ancestors. Nor did breeder associations require "papers" proving a dog was "purebred" and that no mixing with other breeds had occurred anywhere in its ancestry. Rather, terriers, like other kinds of dogs, had been defined not by ancestry but by the region where they evolved and by the job they did, such as hunting, guarding, or herding.

As a type, however, terriers were nevertheless ancient and uniquely English. In 1406 Dame Juliana Berners, Abbess of the Monastery of

St. Albans, included them in her "List of Houndes" (calling them "Teroures")—a compilation of then known English dogs. In 1576 they were described in detail by Dr. John Caius, Queen Elizabeth's personal physician, in his book, *A Treatisse of Englishe Dogges*.

Calling them "terrarius," Caius wrote,

> Another sorte there is which hunteth the Fox and the Badger or Grey onely, whom we call Terrars, because they (after the manner and custome of ferrets in searching for Counyes) creep in the ground, and by that means make afrayde, nyppe and bite the Foxe and the Badger.

In those early days roads were poor, which kept communities isolated from one another. Dogs, like people, had few opportunities to mix with others living at a distance. Propinquity ruled. Dogs were bred to others in their community. So regional differences appeared—differences that, among terriers, would eventually become recognized as distinct breeds (such as Scottish, Welsh, Border, Irish, Lakeland, and Sealyham).

With time, terriers became more specialized as well. By the seventeenth century, they had evolved into two kinds, one short-legged with short hair and the other long-legged with a long, "rough" coat. As the avid foxhunter, Nicholas Cox, explained in his 1687 book *The Gentleman's Recreation*:

> Of Terriers there are two sorts. The one is crooked-legg'd, and commonly short-hair'd: and these will take Earth well, and will lie very long at *Fox* or *Badger*. The other sort is shagged and streight-legg'd: and these will not only hunt above-ground as other Hounds, but also enter the Earth with much more fury than the former; but cannot stay in so long by reason of their great eagerness.

Colors changed, too. Before 1800, most terriers were black and tan. Few were white. But around 1800, breeders, seeking to produce more feisty terriers, began crossing them with bulldogs. As it happened, nearly all bulldogs were white. So gradually, white became a common color among terriers as well. Beagle bloodlines were then added to produce dogs who would yelp or "give voice," when encountering a fox or badger underground, so hunters would know where to find them.

By 1800 such cross-breeding had produced a type of dog that came to be known as the fox terrier. Its long legs made it perfect for chasing foxes over land but were a disadvantage for underground work. Fox terriers who spent too long in a hole suffered terrible cramps and even crippling disabilities.

Russell was fond of fox terriers; and indeed eventually served as a judge of that breed at dog shows. But even as a student at Oxford he realized they needed help underground. When during a chase the fox "went to ground" (i.e., into a hole), foxhunters needed a dog who could "go to ground" (into the hole) and drive their quarry out so the chase could continue. The dog's job, therefore, was not to kill the fox but to keep it above ground. And this required a special kind of terrier—one who could negotiate the smallest fox hole and stay underground for prolonged periods. He should be about the size of a small fox, with a narrow chest so he could squeeze through tight spaces. He should be tough and brave, willing and able to handle a fox if the two should meet face to face in a tunnel. As some fox drains are up to a mile long, he should be able to stay underground for extended periods. And he should be an expert excavator.

Russell loved badger digging and otter hunting as well, and he knew a similar terrier was needed for these sports too. Moreover, as badger and otter were considerably larger and more ferocious than foxes, the dogs that encountered them had to be good fighters and extremely brave.

Badgers are members of the wolverine family and live much of their lives underground, coming up only briefly at night. Growing up to forty pounds, with jaws of vice-like strength, they are the farmers enemy and dangerous to dogs. Preying on small underground rodents as well as chickens, they make big holes in which livestock can and do break their legs. Dogs who encounter them are often killed. The purpose of badger digging was not to destroy these animals but to move them to places where they did less damage. This required terriers to go underground, locate the badger, and keep it occupied while the farmers or hunters dug down and threw a net over it. Only a small, especially brave dog could do this without being killed.

Extremely secretive and nocturnal, like badgers, and about the same size but with an even more lethal bite, otter live in dens along stream banks, behind willows and exposed tree roots. And, although seldom seen, they were nevertheless common in England's streams and did, when too numerous, decimate trout and salmon populations. Hunting them, however, was so difficult that few were ever caught. The sport involved two kinds of dogs—otter hounds to locate the animal and small terriers to chase it out of its den where hunters could net or drown it. This was extremely hazardous work for the dog, as the dens entrances were often under water and required the dog to swim below the surface to enter them and confront their furious quarry.

Where would Russell find such a dog?

* * * * *

One day in May 1819, during his last year as a student at Oxford, Russell found it. His good friend and biographer, E.W.L."Otter" Davies, tells the story:

> Russell was walking towards the Oxford suburb of Marsdon, hoping to devote an hour or two to study in the quiet meads of that hamlet, near the charming slopes of Elsfield, or in the deeper and more secluded haunts of Shotover Wood. But before he had reached Marston a milkman met him with a terrier—such an animal as Russell had as yet only seen in his dreams; he halted, as Actaeon might have done when he caught sight of Diana disporting in her bath; but, unlike that ill-fated hunter, he never budged from the spot till he had won the prize and secured it for his own. She was called Trump, and became the progenitress of that famous race of terriers which, from that day to the present, have been associated with Russell's name at home and abroad—his able and keen coadjutors in the hunting-field.

According to Davies, Trump was

> white with just a patch of dark tan over each eye and ear, while a similar dot, not larger than a penny piece, marks the root of the tail. The coat, which is thick, close, and a trifle wiry, is well calculated to protect the body from wet and cold, but has no affinity with the long, rough jacket of a Scotch terrier. The legs are straight as arrows, the feet perfect; the loins and conformation of the whole frame indicative of hardihood and endurance; while the size and height of the animal may be compared to that of a full-grown vixen fox.

Russell purchased Trump from the milkman on the spot. In his first breeding, he mated Trump with a black and tan terrier that produced a predominantly white dog weighing around fourteen pounds whom Russell named, "Tip." This began a line of small brave terriers perfectly suited to go to ground after badger, otter, and foxes, tunneling sometimes for miles and going so deep they occasionally had to be dug out.

Russell bred Trump and her descendants to any terrier he could find who fit his ideal. He devoted much of the rest of his life, when not foxhunting, to the quest. He scoured Southwest England searching for dogs that approximated the ideal, then bought or borrowed them for breeding. He didn't care about pedigree or papers. He just wanted dogs who could do the job. What he created, therefore, wasn't a "breed" but a type. The Jack Russell was defined not by pedigree but by performance.

In 1948, the English terrier expert Geoffrey Sparrow summarized this philosophy: "The BREED is immaterial, but (a terrier) must be GAME, and by that I mean one that will tackle a fox, badger or otter in his earth whether deep or shallow, wet or dry, and keep at him."

By breeding his terriers for performance, Russell had ensured they would carry the healthiest genes possible. Although he was a founding member of the (English) Kennel Club, he disdained the practice of breeding dogs for show and the inbreeding that goes with it. In contrast to pedigree breeders, Russell kept his studbook open. That would be the secret of the dogs' success. Long before his death, Russell's dogs had become famous throughout England for their intelligence and prodigious feats of courage and endurance.

* * * * *

Love was the secret of the Jack Russell terrier's survival and success. Russell truly adored his dogs, several of which slept on his bed, just as he loved the Devon countryside where he'd spent so much of his life in the saddle. In his heart the two were one. And after his death his devotees' care for him and his dogs kept their spirits alive. A warm and generous man, Russell truly loved—and was loved by—people from all walks of life. He was a hero to the North Devon Gypsies, whom he had rescued from attacks by bigots. He became a close friend of the Prince of Wales, who acquired a portrait of Trump which still hangs in the Harness Room of Sandringham Palace.

When Russell died in 1883 at age eighty-eight, he and his terriers were famous. Both became known for their feats of endurance, as Russell frequently rode thirty or more miles in a day, often with his terriers running beside or sharing the saddle with him. Ever generous, he gave away many of his dogs during his lifetime. After his death, his friends acquired still more.

As legacies, he left not only his beloved terrier but also lasting achievements in conservation. When he began to hunt fox in the second decade of the nineteenth century, foxes were rare in Devon. Whenever a farmer found a fox, he killed it. So Russell and his foxhunting friends dedicated themselves to rescue the species. Russell pleaded with or bribed farmers not to kill foxes. Several of his friends raised foxes for release during hunts. And by the time he died these animals were more plentiful than they had been in a century.

Anyone familiar with the history of conservation would not find this surprising. Hunters, like fishermen, often make good preservationists because they are motivated to save species in which they have a special interest. At the turn of the century an association of hunters, the Boone and Crockett Club, co-founded by the father of American conservation, Teddy Roosevelt, helped save big game species at a time when many of these animals were at risk. Other organizations founded by hunters, such as the National Wildlife Federation and Ducks Unlimited, have achieved similar successes in wildlife conservation.

Today, there are between 250,000 and 450,000 foxes in England who owe their numbers to Reverend Russell, his terriers, their friends and successors.

* * * * *

Alys Serrell was one of those friends. Born in 1842, she grew up as Russell's neighbor. Her father, Henry Digby Serrell, was a friend of Russell's and, like the parson, a clergyman and enthusiastic foxhunter. Over the years, Russell gave the Serrells several terriers and Alys devoted her life to them. When Russell died, she inherited still more, which she bred until 1913. She then gave her dogs to her good friend and neighbor, Augusta Guest, a prominent horsewoman in England's West Country. Eventually Master of Fox Hounds with the famous hunt, the Blackmore Vale, Guest would continue to breed Jack Russells until 1954.

Serrell's 1904 book, *With Hound and Terrier in the Field,* tells us much about the dog. A Jack Russell, she wrote, while friendly to people and a fearless hunter, was not necessarily sociable to its own kind, and three dogs should never be kenneled together, lest two attack and kill the third. The dog "should not be much over 14 inches . . . a size even smaller than this is better . . . A leggy dog is of little or no use for underground work, as, though he may manage to crawl into the earth or drain, he will speedily become so cramped that he can do nothing, and I have seen more than one terrier dug out quite unable to stand."

While it was said Russell never had any but rough-coated (i.e., long-haired) terriers, Serrell kept what were in her day called smooth-coated (i.e., short-haired) ones as well; but even they were rough by today's standards. "In coat," she writes, "the smooth dog cannot be too thick and dense, the slightest appearance of softness being against him, and both smooth and rough should have a good undergrowth, the outer growth of the latter being crisp and hard."

Among Serrell's terriers was Amber, great-granddaughter of Reverend Russell's famous "Tip," who would, she says, "face any wet drain and swim for miles."

> One season she bolted a large fox from a drain under the road near Thornhill, and hanging tight to its brush, she was dragged over a field and to ground in a rabbit-earth before the hounds could get up. She quickly had the fox out again, and he made a meal for the eager pack outside.

> On another occasion she came out of a drain near Holtham so close to her quarry that she collared him in a ditch, and hounds dashing in on the top of them, poor Amber lost half of one of her ears in the fray. This, however, did not make her release her hold of the fox's head, to which she clung so persistently that the huntsman at last cut it off and let her have it.

The "tap-root" of Serrell's kennel was a Jack Russell terrier of indeterminate parentage born in 1880 named "Redcap." At sixteen pounds, she writes, he was "short and compact everywhere with the very best coat that could be—short, hard, and dense—with plenty of undergrowth and thick skin." Yet, despite his small size, Redcap's prodigious feats quickly became local legend.

Once, Serrell writes, she encountered a badger which "was marked to ground in a covert near at hand, and I had Redcap out to try to recover it."

> As soon as the terrier was in, we dug down to them, and choking the terrier off, I tied him to a tree while we set to work to bag the brock, as we thought. He was, however, too quick for us, and bolting out, started off across the open field. As soon as Redcap caught sight of him, he made such a spring at his chain that it snapped, and with about three feet of it dangling behind him the terrier started in pursuit. As he came up to the badger he seized him by the head, and a desperate fight ensued, til at last the badger got his foreleg through the dog's collar, choked him off, and made another run for life. Once again the terrier overtook and pressed him severely, and then, turning suddenly, seized the badger just behind the jaw, and hanging tight to his windpipe, choked him. This badger pulled the scales at 26 lb., and I now have him stuffed in a glass case.

On another occasion Serrell lent Redcap to John Press, a neighbor and retired huntsman of the Blackmore Vale Hounds, to flush foxes who were hiding in a mile-long drain which his other dogs had refused to enter. "The instant Redcap was released in he went. It was not long before a brace of foxes bolted, closely followed by the dog, who then disappeared."

The next morning, Serrell went to her kennels "to see Redcap march out of his box in the orchard, very stiff and dirty, and with the marks of the fray about him." Meanwhile, the neighbor, having thought he'd lost the dog for good, came to apologize. And as he "was sitting on his horse at the bottom of the kennel steps, sadly retelling his history, Redcap suddenly looked at him out of his box, and I shall never forget the change in Press's face as he saw him."

* * * * *

Squire Nicholas Snow, an avid foxhunter who lived next to Exmoor in North Devon, was another who kept the clergyman's strain of terriers alive. As a friend of Russell's, he had, over the years, acquired several of the Parson's terriers. And after Russell died he even hired Russell's own kennel man, Will Rawle, to supervise breeding. Snow's pack, known as "The Stars of the West," became famous throughout England's West Country.

Among Snow's foxhunting friends was a young Cambridge University graduate named Arthur Heinemann, who had come to Devon to study for the ministry and, falling in love with Exmoor, decided to stay. Born in 1871, Heinemann was only twelve when Russell died and never knew the Parson. But he was soon infatuated with the Jack Russell terriers belonging to his friend Snow. Addicted to badger-digging, in 1894 Heinemann founded the West Somerset and Devon Badger-Digging Club to promote the sport and the kind of working terrier he thought best for the job. After moving permanently to Devon in 1902, Heinemann acquired several terriers from Snow and set up his own breeding effort, called the Porlock Kennel. He hired Rawle's granddaughter, Mrs. Annie Harris as "kennelmaid."

Eventually Heinemann, having spent all his money on dogs, went broke. To support himself, he began to write for sporting journals. Then on New Year's Day 1930, he went coursing, fell into a pond, caught pneumonia, and quickly died. He left Porlock Kennel to Mrs. Harris, who continued breeding Jack Russell terriers until the Second World War.

Serrell, Snow, and Heinemann were merely three among many friends who kept Russell's line of terriers alive. Each in this wide circle adopted the Parson's dogs and passed them on to succeeding generations of breeders. All shared Russell's philosophy that his terriers were a type, not a breed, and thus that preserving them required emphasizing performance over pedigree and out-crossing when necessary to achieve this goal. Because those who continued to pursue Russell's ideal were so numerous, their very number—each working independently and not restricted by any kennel club standard—ensured that the genes of this little dog would be far more diverse and healthy than any "purebred."

* * * * *

Russell and these successors, however, were not the only ones to develop a special strain of terrier. Many other English rural sportsmen did as well. Nearly every "MFH" (Master of Fox Hounds) had his or her own idea of the best terrier for the locality depending on soil, weather, kind of quarry, and style of hunting, and who, like Russell himself, experimented with various crosses in their search for the perfect dog for their uses. In Derbyshire, where hunts covered great distances, longer legs were favored. In the wintry lake country, rougher coats predominated. Huntsmen, who were accustomed to carrying the terriers in a saddle-mounted bag until put to ground, preferred shorter dogs.

Given the various needs and conditions and the variety of bloodlines introduced, terrier strains proliferated. Besides types known today, many others, now rare or extinct, appeared as well, such as Jones Terriers, Trumpington Terriers, West Wilts Hunt Terriers, HH Hunt Terriers, Scorrier Terriers, Hucclecote Terriers, North Devon Terriers, Ynysfor Terriers, and Shelburne Terriers.

The genes of many of these eventually found their way into the blood of the Jack Russell as well, producing a dog that came in virtually infinite variations. But whether short or tall; bowed or straight legged; smooth, broken (i.e., inner short and outer long hair), or rough coated; long muzzled or short muzzled; they shared a reputation for bravery and endurance that captured the respect and attention of an entire generation of English sportsmen. In his 1931 book, *Hunt and Working Terriers*, Captain Sir Joselyn Lucas describes some of these feats:

* A local newspaper reported that "a Terrier belonging to the Essex Union Hunt went down an earth after a fox at Ongar and did not return. For six days diggers tried to locate it, and at last succeeded. The exhausted Terrier was given brandy and milk to revive it. Then it tried to get back into the earth again."
* A Jack Russell named "Jack," bred by Arthur Heinemann, once got stuck in a drain with a couple of hounds for sixteen days.

"They had evidently killed their otter," Lucas writes, "as the terrier was badly bitten about the head. All were blind for ten days after they were found, but recovered and hunted for several seasons afterwards."

* A Jack Russell named, "Playfair Snooker," owned by Miss D. Ellis, "went down a drain 250 feet long and had a terrible fight with two badgers. When a large stone slab was lifted, one badger bolted and 'Snooker' drew the other by the scruff of the neck. This is the only time that Miss Ellis has seen a dog draw a badger."

"The badger weighed 29 pounds and the dog nine pounds."

* * * * *

By the Second World War, the Jack Russell—affectionately dubbed a "glorified mutt" by some of its fans—had become a dog for all seasons. After the war its fame and popularity would spread throughout England. When Phineas joined our family, however, few Americans outside foxhunting communities had heard of it. But this was about to change. Within a decade Jack Russells would be broadly popular here as well, and the consequences for them considerable.

6

Growing up Small

*In every location I have ever visited, every hunt is performed
by people whose passion is not for the hunt or the kill, but for
watching the dogs. The hunt is, or has become, sport.*

—Raymond Coppinger,
Dogs

*Not for me the other dogs, running by my side:
Some have run a short while, but none of them would bide.
O Mine is still the lone trail, the hard trail, the best,
Wide wind, and wild starts, and hunger of the quest!*

—Irene Rutherford McLeod,
"Lone Dog," 1915

Phineas grew up small, but refused to admit it. He was short, weighed
around fifteen pounds, and wore a thick, smooth coat. But he thought he
was ten feet tall. He feared nothing and took on any animal he encountered,
from badgers to bears. It was as if, Una being his only canine companion,
he believed himself another Mastiff. Certainly, he and Una were inseparable.
He mimicked her behavior—eating almost as much as she and, because we
insisted Una stay off the furniture and keep "four on the floor," he did the same.
Refusing our laps, he sat at our feet looking up at us with a soulful expression
that seemed to say, "I'm dying to sit in your lap but am too proud."

And no job was too big for Phineas. Each morning he and Una greeted
the dawn by chasing the coyotes that paraded past our buildings. He accompanied Diana everywhere she rode, killing marmots, chasing bears,
and confronting skunks and porcupines. He played with Little Orphan
Annie and joined my treks down Suicide in search of trout.

He had nine lives and needed every one. He wasn't afraid to swim
across the Smith and once nearly drowned. He took on thirty-pound

51

Phineas, December 1977
"He thought he was ten feet tall."

badgers with jaws like wood chippers. He regularly challenged coyotes to games of "chicken." Once in winter he fell off a fifty-foot cliff, surviving unharmed when he landed in deep snow, the impact sending his little body six feet under.

And never had we known such a hunter! Our pastures were over-run with Richardson ground squirrels, a little rodent Montanans incorrectly call "gophers," which do terrible damage to the land. To construct their underground dens, they dig up the grass, thereby creating opportunities for noxious weeds—hound's tongue, musk and Canadian Thistle, knapweed, and leafy spurge—to take over. Badgers in search of a meal excavate the gophers' dens, turning the rodents' small holes into big ones which sometimes trip horses and cows, breaking bones. And indeed, in 1975, Diana's beloved thoroughbred, Antinomy broke her leg in such a hole and had to be put down. We grieved over Antinomy's loss and fretted about the danger and damage these little rodents caused, but as we wouldn't use poison, there seemed little to be done to control their numbers.

Until Phineas. He became our Orkin man, dispatching gophers more efficiently than any other predator. A coyote, for example, hunts gophers, but inefficiently. It waits patiently without moving at a gopher's hole and pounces when the little rodent comes out to sun itself at the den entrance. By contrast, Phineas had no patience. He simply ran flat out through the fields, leaping in the air every three strides high enough to see above the grass and spot gophers ahead. Moving like the wind, he was on his quarry in an instant, catching and killing it with a shake, then moving on to the next without slowing down.

Many evenings we accompanied Phineas on his hunting expeditions in our Land Cruiser. This was our spectator sport. As we drove to the front gate and back, a round trip of four miles, Phineas ran parallel to us, perhaps a hundred feet away. We watched with fascination as he flew across the landscape, bounding in the air at warp speed, snatching and killing a gopher then flying forward to the next kill. At the end of the run he'd taken twenty or more.

Despite the many other wonderful dogs who'd blessed our lives, we'd never known another like Phineas. There was something wild and sad about him. His was a free spirit, a feral dog who kept his distance. Growing up tiny in a big country full of dangers, he looked so vulnerable we felt an urge to coddle him. But he wouldn't let us. He craved love but couldn't accept it. He was too proud. And that made us love him all the more.

* * * * *

Phineas settled into the routine of our lives. He slept with Una by our bed on the frigid Manse floor. At dawn, he joined Una's ritual encounter with the coyotes. After chasing them over the hill, Una leading the way, they returned, panting and quite pleased with themselves, to the kitchen house. After breakfast, Una and I left Diana and Phineas in the Kitchen House to slog through the snow to the Hobby House, where I wrote through early afternoon. Shortly before dark Diana and I filled and lit the Coleman and Kerosene lanterns and lined them in a row on the table behind the couch, where, after dinner, we read until the wood stove and lanterns depleted the cabin's oxygen and drowsiness overcame us.

Isolation remained our companion. As our building lay in a radio dead spot at the bottom of the coulee, I put an antenna on a fencepost high in the pasture near the Packdown and installed a two-way radio in the Land Cruiser. In emergencies I could then drive to the antenna, run a wire to the vehicle's radio, and call our Great Falls answering service, which would patch us through to a telephone line. And although in winter it sometimes took two hours or more to shovel through snowdrifts to reach the antenna, at least we had a lifeline.

As more insurance, we acquired two snowmobiles. We kept the Land Cruiser at the ranch, the four-wheel drive Ford pickup at the Andersons' in Millegan, and an old Datsun pickup with the Carliles in Hound Creek. When the ranch became snowbound, we snowmobiled to the Anderson's; and if they were snowbound too, continued the additional twenty-five miles to the Carliles', from which we drove the Datsun to Great Falls.

That same fall we borrowed the money to buy a tiny house in town we called "the Telephone Booth," and which we used almost exclusively for that purpose. We no longer needed the airport pay phones and could actually sit down to have a phone conversation. Nevertheless, making calls took three days—one via snowmobile and truck to reach town, a second to make the calls, and a third to return to the ranch.

The seclusion and struggle accelerated our friendship with Phineas. When I fought my way through snowdrifts to the radio antenna, he frequently came along; when we snowmobiled to Great Falls, he rode shotgun; and when we stayed at the phone booth, he was there. Even that first fall, while just three months old, he joined our daily pilgrimages to the Point; and when winter came and weather permitted, he accompanied us on walks to the Packdown and back. When spring arrived, he took longer treks with Una and me. We climbed down Suicide Trail to the Smith, where I fished until dark; or walked up the slopes of Gaddis and into the nearly impenetrable recesses of Black Canyon on the other side, to visit the prehistoric cave paintings.

* * * * *

As the dogs and I continued our explorations, their purpose subtly changed. In the past, when the snow melted and light green leaves first showed on the aspen, I usually thought of fishing. I'd be eager to hike to the river to greet the trout after a winter's absence. Hiking had been incidental—a means to get fishing. But after Phineas' arrival, the means became the ends. Rather than walk to fish, I fished as an excuse to walk—and watch Phineas hunt on the way. Diana's rides underwent a similar transformation, as the little dog subtly reversed their purpose.

Phineas drew us more deeply into the land. And so we walked and rode, going higher into the mountains now, rather than down to the river. One day merged seamlessly into the next as we explored the high country. The simple pattern of our lives and the predictable repetitions of the seasons combined with the unchanging landscape to convey a sense of *deja vu*, until one glorious May day when time seemed to disappear altogether.

Phineas, Una, and I walked to the top of Gaddis, then westward onto the neighboring Dana Ranch, to the top of a broad ridge that divided the Smith River and Hound Creek drainages. Below us, Hound Creek meandered through a broad valley of tall grass bisected by small tributaries, and further out rose the Big Belt Mountains, layer after layer of pastel ridges as far as the eye could see. To the east, the red rocky lips of the Smith River canyon jutted like an open wound across the land, and beyond them Tenderfoot Creek and the Little Belt Mountains blended into the horizon. No soul breathed or building stood within twenty miles to break our solitude.

Alone with our thoughts, we descended in silence past a derelict homestead next to a bubbling spring. What happened to the family who lived there, I wondered? They probably had children and a dog or cat. Almost certainly, living so far from medical attention, they experienced death—perhaps a son or daughter in childbirth, cat by leukemia or dog eaten by wolves, or all of the above. Then one day they probably went broke—the breadwinner died, perhaps, or their cattle decimated by a succession of bad winters—and the survivors left Millegan for good. What did they feel, I wondered, when they looked back on this magnificent land for the last time?

Ahead stood the large rock outcropping we called, "Bullethole," with three small caves running through the entire bluff, as though drilled by a giant auger. Contrasted with the homesteaders' short lives, Bullethole stood immobile and unchanging, a reminder of eternity.

I thought about Thomas Mann's masterful, 1924 novel, *The Magic Mountain*, about Hans Castorp, a young man from Hamburg, Germany who before World War I traveled to Davos, Switzerland, high in the Alps to visit a cousin who was being treated for tuberculosis at a sanatorium there. Castorp intended to stay three weeks, but ultimately remained seven years.

The novel is rich with themes about life, and one of them concerns time. Hamburg is busy and hectic. By contrast, life on the Magic Mountain is quiet and meditative. As Castorp's journey takes him from busy Hamburg to quiet Davos a funny thing happens—time disappears. Mann is reminding readers that we measure time by movement—the movement of the hands of a clock, or of the planets, stars or electrons—and the changes or passages in our lives. Where nothing moves time becomes immeasurable and we lose sense of its passing.

And so in Millegan, where every day was repetition. The routine of our lives, the cycle of the seasons, never varied. One day blended imperceptibly with the next. Millegan was our Magic Mountain. Time stood still.

Or were we suffering from an illusion? *Which* was real—time and the busy world of Hamburg and New York, or something lying beyond time that we now glimpsed in here, in the mountains?

* * * * *

The notion that time does not exist is not new. In fact, it is a common theme that has run through the history of philosophy for millennia, and is shared by some of the greatest minds who ever lived. The Greek philosopher, Parmenides, who flourished around 500 B.C., argued that change and motion were illusions and "what is" (i.e., reality) "is without beginning, indestructible, entire, single, unshakable, endless."

A century later, Plato said something similar. While the objects around us seem to be born, change, move, grow, decay, and die, he said, they are not real. They are mere copies of real things, which he called, "Forms." Forms are the archetypes of which the objects of our experience are imitations. And Forms are unchanging, eternal, non-material, and invisible to the senses. Being unchanging, they exist beyond time. What we experience as time, he suggests, is merely the "moving likeness of eternity."

Philosophers call thinkers such as Plato, "idealists," not because they had higher ideals than others, but because they believed ultimate reality consists of non-physical things like spirits and ideas. One kind of idealist was the seventeenth-century Dutch philosopher Benedict Spinoza. The first step to understanding, he argued, was to perceive the universe "*sub specie aeternitatus*"—"under the aspect of eternity." That is not to say, Spinoza explained, that reality is "everlasting"—i.e., that it exists in time but never ends. Rather it means that reality is *beyond time*. The concept of temporality simply doesn't apply to it. Time is an illusion—what Spinoza called, an "aid to the imagination." To really know a thing is to contemplate it beyond time.

Perhaps the greatest idealist philosopher who ever lived was Immanuel Kant, an eighteenth-century German whose work profoundly influenced the famed twentieth-century physicist Albert Einstein. "Time is not something that exists in itself," Kant wrote in his 1781 treatise, *The Critique of Pure Reason*, but "a purely subjective condition of our (human) intuition . . . and in itself, apart from the subject, is nothing." That we see things in time, in other words, is a reflection of our inability to conceive them beyond time. But that doesn't mean time exists. It only means we can't imagine things not in time.

When I was a college student Kant convinced me, thereby also inspiring me to choose philosophy as a career. But I soon found idealism had fallen out of favor with most philosophers. At the universities where I pursued graduate study, they held space, time, and the physical world to be the only realities and that questioning their reality merely revealed oneself to be suffering from a kind of philosophical neurosis. The proper job of philosophy, they believed, was to cure people of this illness—to be philosophical psychoanalysts helping them overcome the terrible affliction of idealism. Eventually they persuaded me too, but in doing so killed my interest. Their conception of philosophy had no appeal and accelerated my decision to abandon it as a career.

But this glorious spring day, as Una, Phineas, and I descended Gaddis, I wondered: What if the idealists were right all along? Then our world would be infused with new possibilities and nothing—neither our or the dogs' lives—would ever be the same again.

* * * * *

"He who embarks on the career of Master of Hounds is like to find that sport runs away with the cash." So wrote a prominent foxhunter in 1674. It wasn't surprising then that the Reverend Russell was perennially short of money and died pennyless. He spent all he had on dogs and horses and riding with them across the beautiful, open spaces of Devon. Yet he never regretted his life. The companionship of animals and the countryside more than justified penury. Likewise, Heinemann went bankrupt and was forced to pursue a career as a writer to fund his obsession for Jack Russell terriers and badger digging.

Now it was our turn. Like Russell and Heinemann Diana and I spent everything on animals and the land. And like them, we were going broke. Throughout the spring of 1978 I wrote prolifically and collected rejection slips. We sank deeper into debt. But, like these Englishmen, we could not bring ourselves to worry. Was it because, living in the country we saw our lives *sub specie aeternitatus*—that we realized contemplating the river or watching Phineas run was closer to reality than worrying whether credit card payments were made by the middle of the month?

I don't know why we didn't worry, but we didn't. Like Mr. Micawber in Charles Dickens' *Pickwick Papers* we told ourselves, "Something will turn up."

And it did. The breakthrough came in June 1978 when *The Atlantic Monthly* decided to publish my reflections on the decline of liberal arts education. Entitled "Skipping through College," it would be the cover article in the September issue. We received a copy in August.

A week after we heard from *The Atlantic*, Zoomie disappeared. In the middle of one night, he came into Lawrance's tent, apparently frightened by something, then left forever, almost certainly killed by a mountain lion, lynx, or bobcat.

If this was an omen, we failed to notice. Instead, when a friend invited me on a backpacking trip into in the Beartooth Mountains over the Labor Day weekend, I accepted.

"Don't worry about me," Diana said as we left. "The dogs and horses are good company. We'll be fine."

7

The Soul of a Dog

So I laugh when I hear them make it plain
That dogs and men never meet again.
For all their talk who'd listen to them
With the soul in the shining eyes of him?
Would God be wasting a dog like Tim?

—Winifred M. Letts,
"Tim an Irish Terrier"

The lower animals share with man the attributes of
Reason, Language, Memory, a sense of Moral Re-
sponsibility, Unselfishness, and Love, all of which
belong to the spirit and not to the body; and...there
is every reason to presume that the lower animals
may share his immortality hereafter as they share
his mortality at present.

—Rev. J. G. Wood,
Man and Beast, Here and Hereafter, *1893*

Labor Day 1978 dawned cloudless. But a cool breeze brought a hint of fall to the air as Diana stood in the corral, saddling Dandy. It was a perfect day, she thought, to ride the Packdown to the river, then return through the narrow and forested Two Creek Canyon. Of course, she'd take Phineas and Una. But where *was* Phineas?

Suddenly an awful sound, something between a moan and a scream, pierced the air, chilling Diana. Then Phineas ran into the corral, crying in obvious pain. Wild with panic he darted for the granary and began crawling under it. Diana lunged, caught him by his stubby tail, and pulled him out.

She put him on the seat beside her in the Land Cruiser and headed for the veterinarian in Great Falls. He continued to pant and cry.

"Hang in there," she pleaded.

But before she'd driven three miles, he was dead.

When my friend and I returned from the Beartooth the next day Diana greeted us in tears. We took Phineas' body to the vet for an autopsy but it was too late for an accurate examination and he couldn't find the cause. Probably he ate poisoned bait a trapper had left for the coyotes. But we would never know. All that mattered was that he was gone.

Phineas had been with us less than a year. We had not wanted a little dog. Yet in just those few months, he had stolen our hearts forever. In life, he seemed beyond reach, craving our love but somehow unable to accept it. His was a free spirit, and we couldn't believe such a soul could ever really die.

"God wouldn't have wasted a wonderful dog like Phineas, letting him die so young," Diana said. "I've got to believe he's is still happy and alive somewhere, in Heaven maybe, scampering through the Elysian Fields, and that someday we'll join him."

I wanted to believe too, but couldn't. Yet in our grief we could not stop hoping. Was not the immortality of dogs at least a possibility? Phineas' death would launch us on a thirty-year quest for the answer. For, while Diana's optimism initially failed to raise my own spirits, I still saw a glimmer of hope. And the source of this light was the philosophy I once believed but had been persuaded to reject, namely idealism.

* * * * *

"Animals share with us the privilege of having a soul," wrote the Greek philosopher Pythagoras in the sixth century, B.C. A century later, another Greek, Hippocrates, observed "the soul is the same in all living creatures, although the body of each is different." Plato thought much the same thing. And so have many idealist philosophers throughout history, for the same reasons they believed time does not exist. Reality, being spiritual and eternal, included souls both human and animal.

These philosophers came to this conclusion in part through their understanding of mathematics. Geometry and arithmetic concern things like numbers, points, and lines. These mathematical entities clearly exist, they believed, because mathematics helps us understand reality. By using math, physics unlocks the secrets of the universe. And how could mathematics, which concerns abstractions like numbers, explain reality unless reality, too, were immaterial?

"Was not the immortality of dogs at least a possibility? Phineas, death would launch us on a thirty-year quest for the answer."

Consider the number one: It's immaterial and unchanging. There is only one number one. As the carol, "The Twelve Days of Christmas," puts it, "One is one and all alone and ever more shall be so." But the number one shouldn't be confused with the numerals that represent it, such as the Arabic "1" and the Roman, "I." There's an infinite number of numeral ones. Every time we mark "1" on a page or blackboard, we've created another. Such are physical and visible and can be readily reproduced (by making another mark on paper or blackboard) or destroyed (burning the paper, erasing the blackboard).

In short, numbers are the real thing and numerals their copies—a difference not unlike the distinction between reality and virtual reality. The virtual world created by computers is a copy, or model, of the real world, not real itself.

To Plato, for example, reality consists of Forms, which are invisible, immaterial and timeless. There's a Form for everything, not merely mathematical objects, and to have real knowledge of anything at all requires directly apprehending the Form of which it is a copy. But since we cannot see Forms with our own eyes, we must "see" them in some non-physical way, too, and must belong to the same immaterial world as the Forms. We call this non-physical part our soul.

That's one reason why Plato believed in immortality. He'd say every living thing, including Phineas, possesses a soul, which like the Forms is unchanging, ethereal, and invisible. So while his body, like all bodies, eventually perishes his soul never does.

* * * * *

For such early philosophers these arguments settled the issue: all living things are immortal. But unlike the ancients, some in the Christian era insisted that only humans are. The seventeenth-century French philosopher Rene Descartes, for example, espoused a doctrine known as dualism—that each person was composed of a body and an immaterial soul (which he called, "mind") that controlled the body and that resided in the pineal gland, a small organ situated at the base of the brain. But animals, he claimed, have no pineal gland and therefore have no place to keep a soul. Besides, he added, the reason humans have souls is so that they can be held morally accountable for their actions on Judgment Day. But animals aren't held morally accountable for their acts. They are, he said, amoral.

Of course, this was nonsense, as other philosophers quickly pointed out. If the soul is not physical, they noted, it can't reside in the pineal gland or any other physical location. Besides, other animals (including dogs) do have pineal glands! If humans have souls, then other animals, including dogs, do as well. The differences between us and them are merely of degree. As a contemporary of Descartes, the English playwright Thomas Nash observed in 1600, dogs are superior.

> Yet, in a jest, since thou rail'st so 'gainst dogs,
> I'll speak a word or two in their defense.
> That creature's best that comes most near to men;
> That dogs of all come nearest, thus I prove:
> First, they excell us in all outward sense,
> Which no one of experience will deny:
> They hear, they smell, they see better than we.
> To come to speech, they have it questionless,
> Although we understand them not so well,
> They bark as good old Saxon as may be,
> And that in more variety than we.

By the nineteenth century, most scientists and philosophers believed animals and men closely resembled each other. "There is no fundamental difference between man and the high mammals in their mental faculties," Charles Darwin wrote:

> . . . the difference in mind between man and the higher animals, great as it is, certainly is one of degree and not of kind. The love for all living creatures is the most noble attribute of man. We have seen that the senses and intuitions, the various emotions and faculties, such as love, memory, attention and curiosity, imitation, reason, etc., of which man boasts may be found in an incipient, or even sometimes a well-developed condition, in the lower animals.

"One must be really quite blind or totally chloroformed," the German philosopher Arthur Schopenhauer observed in 1840, "not to recognize that the essential and principal thing in the animal and man are the same." The only difference between humans and other animals, said Schopenhauer, is that humans have a more developed capacity for abstract reason. But that difference, he says, is only a matter of degree, and not important.

"The similarity between animal and man," he explained, "is incomparably greater" than this difference. For humans' capacity for abstract reason is not the source of their supposed moral superiority. Rather it stems from the ability to feel compassion for other living things. And animals feel this compassion too. Hence, humans have no monopoly on virtue and "the eternal being, as it lives in us, also lives in every animal."

Later, science would confirm this close affinity. About 75 percent of men's and dogs' genes, we now know, are identical. Of the 24,567 genes possessed by humans, 18,473 have a canine equivalent. Far from being "less evolved," dogs are as complex as humans. A dog genome contains 2.4 billion base pairs, a human 2.9 billion. Dogs have 78 chromosomes in every cell, humans just 46.

But even as science came to see the similarities between people and animals, it denied the immortality of both. Philosophers, persuaded by science, rejected idealism and dualism. Only what we directly experience, they argued (i.e., observable, physical events in time) are real and only theories that can be "verified" by these events are true. So numbers are not real but rather just figments of mathematicians' imaginations—theoretical concepts governed by the rules of hypothetical games scientists play to build testable models of reality. Likewise, souls don't exist either. To believe they inhabit our—or our dogs'—bodies is to succumb to what one modern philosopher called, "the myth of the ghost in the machine." But ghosts don't exist, these philosophers said. Only bodies exist, but they are merely machines. When they die, we die. Death is final.

Science and philosophy, therefore, seemed to put an end to idealism and the hope for immortality. And as a scholar and philosopher of science I, too, had to conclude that there is no afterlife.

* * * * *

Yet I began to wonder: Could this conclusion be wrong? Could there be a purely scientific explanation for immortality? The geneticist, Richard Dawkins, called genes "immortal." Did the key to Phineas' immortality lie in science after all? Was there something that might be called, "genetic immortality?"

As usual, Diana read my thoughts. "Do you think we could find another dog exactly like Phineas?" she asked.

It seemed unlikely, I said. Each human is utterly unique. Even identical twins share only half their genes. Yet genetically speaking, dogs are every bit as complicated as humans. The canine genome contains billions of base pairs. That translates into more possible combinations of traits than all the atoms in the universe. And Phineas died without issue. So finding another like him was a statistical impossibility.

"In other words," Diana replied, "it would take a miracle. But miracles sometimes happen, don't they?"

Indeed, they do. We resolved to call the Boltons and to see if Phineas had a brother.

8

Hamilton Farm

*The Star Ridge Hunt, of which Mr. Erastus Tefft is Master, hunt
a roughish country in New York, State...his (Jack Russell) terriers came over with the first draft. (The hunt was established
in 1928.) Mr. Tefft likes his terriers as small as possible, for the
usual earths are enlarged woodchuck holes, deserted by their
former owners. . . . The terriers are carried on horseback.*

*According to the late Arthur Heinemann, whose Jack Russells
were so famous, the parson ...incorporated into his pack any
terrier that . . . came up to his standards of make and shape and
work. He goes on to say that he and other breeders who have
tried to maintain the Jack Russell standard have had to bring in
fresh blood from time to time or the strain would be too hope-
lessly inbred.*

—Captain Sir Jocelyn M. Lucas,
Bart, Hunt and Working Terriers, *1931*

The snow glistened in the bright February sunlight. Steam, drawn by
the cold, rose slowly from the river below. Outside the cockpit, even the
air looked stiff as ice. Through my headset, over the loud throbbing of
the helicopter engine I heard the rancher tell the pilot, "Take a pass along
Two Creek. There's usually some hang out there."

"Real cold out," the pilot replied. "Pelts should be pretty good."

Resting his hunting rifle across his lap, the rancher scanned the field below
with binoculars. Squeezed between him and the pilot I felt like an army medic
in an ambulance on my way to pick up wounded during combat. Mumtazi
remained at the ranch, snowbound and starving. To rescue her I'd hitched
this helicopter ride with the rancher, who had agreed to drop me off there.

But on the way he planned to hunt coyotes. To save a life I might witness death. I found myself wondering, "How did I get myself into this?"

* * * * *

A week after Phineas died, Diana and I called the Boltons. Yes, Perry said, he and Aurelia hoped to breed Fenwick to Adelaide, Phineas' parents, again this fall. So if all went well another litter would arrive around December 1st. And if so, we could have a pup.

The fall passed glacially as we waited for news from the Maryland whelping bed. In the meantime, our little family of animals continued to shrink. The next to go was Little Orphan Annie. The wild coyotes made clear from the beginning that they did not like her. In their eyes, she was an intruder. Each evening before dark they walked slowly by the Kitchen House, "showing the flag" by ominously staring in her direction. Gradually these menacing parades came closer and closer to the Kitchen House where Annie quivered in fear below the deck.

Then one morning Annie was gone—vanished. We never saw her again. The wild coyotes had surely killed her.

On November 30th, the Boltons called to say Adelaide had whelped the day before, and they were reserving a male pup for us. The little guy looked like Phineas, they said, and would be eight weeks old and ready to go February 1st. We immediately decided to call him "Finn."

This time, however, we told the Boltons that rather than ship the dog to us I'd pick him up in Maryland and bring him home myself. After "Skipping through College" appeared in September, the *Atlantic Monthly Press* asked me to write a book on higher education. I acquired a New York literary agent. So in January I'd take a research trip east, stopping briefly to see my publisher in Boston, agent in New York, and friends in Morristown, New Jersey and Washington. As the Boltons lived near Washington, I'd pick up Finn and take him home with me.

But buying dogs creates momentum of its own. Once one starts, it's hard to stop. Having lost Phineas, we told ourselves, "You can't have too many dogs. If you have just one or two, when one dies, the pain of loss is too great. Better have several, as emotional insurance." So after hearing from the Boltons we immediately bought another dog to keep Finn and Una company, a mastiff puppy we named "Basil." Having exceeded the threshold of one dog, we couldn't stop.

In mid-January we left Mumtazi in the Bath House with two weeks supply of food and plenty of water and took the other animals to Great Falls, so they could stay with Diana in the Telephone Booth while I was away. And the next day I caught a plane for points east. All went according to plan until, after visiting Boston and New York, I arrived in Morristown on Saturday, February 3rd to see my friends, Bill and Ejie Dana. That evening Diana called from the Phone Booth to say ferocious storms were sweeping Millegan. They completely closed the road. She worried about Mumtazi, who was out of food. But there was no sense for me to hurry back. If she couldn't get to the ranch, I couldn't either. We'd have to wait for a break in the weather.

So we decided to stick to the original itinerary. I'd complete my visits in New Jersey and Washington and pray Mumtazi could hold on until there was a break in the weather.

* * * * *

The next day drenching rain slapped against the windows as Bill Dana and I sat in his study, reading Sunday's *New York Times*.

"What do you want to do this morning?" Ejie asked. "You can't hide behind the newspaper all day."

"I dunno," I replied. "What's there to do on a rainy February Sunday morning in New Jersey?"

"We could visit the National Equestrian Center," she suggested. "That's where the U.S. Olympic Equestrian Team trains."

"Um," I answered without enthusiasm.

"There's a famous Jack Russell Terrier kennel there called Hamilton Farm," she went on. "We could visit that."

"Where's my raincoat?" I replied.

* * * * *

Hamilton Farm, I would learn, played a preeminent role in the introduction of Jack Russell terriers to America.

The first dogs came from England and Ireland, brought by private individuals at the beginning of the twentieth century. Annie Harris and Augusta Guest sold dogs to people all over the world, including some Americans. And most of these were brought by foxhunters.

Hunting communities in America and England formed a transatlantic culture. Englishmen and women occasionally rode to hounds as guests of American friends, and *vice versa*. So American hunters quickly discovered Jack Russells and began acquiring them.

In 1919, for example, an experienced English terrier breeder named S. T. Holland began raising short-legged, rough-coated Jack Russell terriers—including one he had acquired from Mrs. Harris—and some found their way to America. In 1930, one named "Tiger" was acquired by the Chagrin Valley Hunt in Ohio, which then began breeding Jack Russells on its own.

Like their English counterparts, Americans were impressed with the courage and ability of the little dogs. In 1928 one bitch named "Flossie" so astounded Erastus Tefft, Master of the Starr Ridge (New York) Hunt, that he told Lucas she "seems devoid of physical sensation when at work."

"Mr. Tefft," reports Lucas, "says he has seen her dragged out by the heels, when put to dig out a big dog (male) fox, hauled out with the fox and a vixen so fastened together that they could hardly be separated. Blood spurted from the two big holes in the top of her nose, but she minded not at all, and was wild to go back again." This is only one of many instances of the pluck of this tiny terrier and her get.

Again like the English, these Americans experimented with out-crosses to produce terriers best suited to local conditions. Although, like Russell, American MFHs preferred dogs with rough or broken coats, which gave the best protection in cold weather; they also tended to prefer, more often than the English, short-legged dogs.

The reason, as one early American foxhunter, MFH of the Shelbourne, Vermont, hunt, J. Watson Webb explained, was because in the eastern United States badgers were quite rare and foxes tended to live in woodchuck holes. By contrast, in England, where badgers were plentiful, foxes lived in holes originally made by badgers, which are larger. Hence, according to Webb, many English terriers, being bred to go into Badger holes, "are too large to be of much use to us here." So in 1911 he began cross-breeding, eventually producing a smaller terrier he called the "Shelbourne, a small, game breed suitable for our hunting."

In this way, hunt terriers in America, including Jack Russells, exhibited great diversity. Like their English sporting counterparts, they were defined by their temperament and ability, not appearance. There was no such thing as typical conformation. A Jack Russell's height could vary from ten to fifteen inches, its hair from short ("smooth"), medium ("broken"), or long ("rough"). While most had white coats randomly decorated with variously-sized patches of black or brown, some had lots of color while others had none.

* * * * *

Somewhere during this history, Jack Russells came to Hamilton Farm. Early in the twentieth century, a wealthy financier named James Cox Brady built this large country estate in Somerset County, New Jersey, near Far Hills, naming it after his wife's family. He bred prize-winning livestock and built a lavish fifty-horse stable in which he raised a wide variety of horses, from Clydesdales to thoroughbred hunters. He also built an elegant dog kennel and began importing prize German Shepherd dogs from Germany, which he bred and showed.

And he may also have imported Jack Russell terriers. An intriguing 1912 photograph of Brady found by his granddaughter, Mrs. Harden L. (Ailsa) Crawford, shows him in his kennel surrounded with Jack Russells. But whether those dogs were actually his and what happened to them is not known.

In 1933 ownership of Hamilton Farm passed to Brady's former brother-in-law, the naturalist, C. Suydham Cutting. During a visit to Tibet in 1930, the Dali Lama gave Cutting some unusual small dogs, known as Lhasa Apsos, which Cutting took home to America. Soon he and his wife were breeding them at Hamilton Farm.

By the 1950s Hamilton Farm had passed to Ailsa Crawford. And not long after, Mrs. Crawford had a fateful encounter with a Jack Russell terrier. She had been visiting a good friend and neighbor, Mrs. Nelson Slater, MFH of the Essex Hunt near Far Hills. Mrs. Slater always kept many dogs, but when Mrs. Crawford entered the Slater's house it was a small terrier that made the biggest impression: A tiny two-year old Jack Russell named "Rare" (pronounced "rarie").

It was love at first sight. Rare so enchanted Mrs. Crawford that Mrs. Slater gave her the dog on the spot.

Rare quickly revealed herself to be braver and brighter than any dog Mrs. Crawford had ever known. Soon after arriving at Hamilton Farm, however, Rare disappeared. She looked everywhere for her without success. Eventually, she noticed a hole under the floor of their front porch. Reaching into the opening, she could only feel, she told me, "a bunch of legs." And when she pulled on this tangle of limbs, out popped Rare still attached to a fox, which was nearly dead. After Rare had been pried from her prize, the little dog dove right back down the hole in hopes of finding another fox.

Ailsa Crawford was hooked. From then on she would devote herself to Jack Russells. She took annual trips to England, bringing back new stock for breeding. In 1976 she founded the Jack Russell Terrier Club of America (JRTCA), dedicated to preserving "the unique characteristics and working heritage of this great little terrier."

But it wouldn't last. In May 1978, the Crawfords' house burned to the ground, killing one of their daughters. Grieving, Ailsa Crawford turned the management of the kennel over to Marilyn Veile, whose husband was chief groom for the US Equestrian Center, also located at the estate. In a few years the Hamilton Farm Jack Russell kennel would cease operation altogether and Mrs. Veile would have the chore of finding homes for the last dogs.

But in the meantime, Ejie Dana and I would go there to find a very special Jack Russell waiting for me.

* * * * *

It was still raining hard when Ejie and I arrived at the kennel—a low building that sat to the left of the driveway. Mrs. Veile met us at the door and led us into a large, barn-like room, divided by a center isle lined with whelping pens, each pen containing three to five JR pups, plus their mothers.

The pups peered at us intently over their cubicle dividers, without making a sound. For a moment, the eerie silence held. Then suddenly all dogs began barking at once. All, that is, except one, who silently locked her gaze on me and wouldn't let go. As I approached her, this fuzzy little nine-week-old fur ball pushed past the other pups, grabbed the top edge of the divider with her paws, hoisted herself up, and insisted I hold her.

There was something strange and mysterious about this little girl. She clearly wasn't related to the others in the pen or to their mother, also in the pen, and who seemed to consider her an outsider. Neither Alisa Crawford nor Marilyn Veile could tell me much about her -- other than to say she wasn't a "Hamilton Farm" Jack Russell (a cachet that carried considerable snob appeal). So why was she there alone?

It would be twenty-eight years before I met John Ike, the man who owned her mother, Holly, and who partly solved the mystery. She was—if dogs can be such things—a love child. According to Ike, he had left Holly, an outstanding dog whose father, Rufus MacNeil, came from Ireland, to board at Hamilton Farm while he was away on business. While there, Holly was accidentally bred by a terrier whose identity would never be clear. When Ike returned to find Holly pregnant, he asked Marilyn to find the pups a home. But there would only be one, whom Marilyn would name "Holly's Folly" and who would be waiting for me when I arrived at Hamilton Farm.

It was love at first sight. With a long white coat and a brown and black patch over one eye, she resembled an earmuff. Yet, although nearly every other dog in the kennel was better looking, she stood out as though a spotlight followed her every move.

"I've just got to have her," I told Ejie.

"What'll Diana say?" she asked.

"That may be a problem," I answered. Even Diana, of course, would think I'd gone nuts.

Back at the Danas' I took a deep breath and called Diana.

"I visited the country's leading Jack Russell kennel today," I said, hoping that would impress her. "It's called Hamilton Farm. They have the cutest little rough-coat female Jack Russell, born on November 28th, one day before Finn. What do you think about getting her? Then we could raise pups and never run out of Jack Russells again."

"She sounds wonderful," Diana replied, cautiously. "But Alston, perhaps we should be sensible for a change. We just got Basil and he's barely housebroken. You're picking up Finn on Friday. Mumtazi's in trouble at the ranch. You've got a book to write. I think we should pass on this one."

How could I argue? Unfortunately, she was the voice of reason. "You're right," I replied morosely.

As we talked Bill Dana sat next to me, smoking his pipe, listening. "She is right, you know," he said thoughtfully, after I'd hung up. "You've got plenty on your plate. It wouldn't be wise to take on another pup at this time."

Everyone was so reasonable it made me feel miserable. Then the phone rang.

It was Diana.

"Buy her!" she said.

I immediately called Mrs. Veile.

* * * * *

"Alston, have you gone completely bonkers?" Ruth Daniloff asked as we sat with her husband Nick in the living room of their Washington house. "You've already got two dogs and this lady from Baltimore is delivering you a pup this afternoon. That's three. And you tell me you're already committed to getting a fourth? What's going on? You used to be so sensible."

"I was never sensible," I replied. "I just pretended to be. As far as animals are concerned, I've always been irresponsible. You're just noticing it for the first time, that's all. Isn't that so, Nick?"

Nick, one of my oldest friends, sat in the corner with a Cheshire cat smile on his face. "Yes Ruth, he's right. He's always been a flake. He's just coming out of the closet now."

Diana and Finn, Spring 1978
"'He's a little lover,'
Mrs. Bolton said as she got back into her car."

"But I still don't understand," Ruth persisted. "How will you get this New Jersey dog to Montana?"

"The kennel manager, Mrs. Veile, is bringing the pup to me at National Airport tomorrow morning," I explained. "When I called her last Sunday to say I wanted the pup but couldn't take it then because I was leaving for Washington the next day she offered to fly it down from Newark and meet me at National before my plane leaves for Montana. And so she is, at no charge."

"How lucky she cares more about pups than profits," Ruth said. "So you're taking both home as carry-on luggage in a pet carrier? That'll be interesting."

Just then, as if on cue, Aurelia Bolton arrived at the door with a tiny terrier. At first glance, the pup looked just like Phineas—same long nose and solemn eyes. And size. But when I took him into my arms, differences became apparent. While the spots on Phineas' face and back were mostly black, Finn's were brown, and where Phineas tensed when touched, the new pup melted into my arms.

"He's a little lover," Mrs. Bolton said, as she got back into her car. But I'd already discovered that. At bedtime, he climbed under the covers with me and didn't budge the whole night.

The next morning, I said to Finn, "We've just had a bonding experience."

But he already knew that.

* * * * *

Mrs. Veile was waiting when Ruth and I arrived at National Airport Saturday morning. Inside a crate she carried the little pup, quiet as a mouse. What are you going to call her, Mrs. Veile asked.

"Ifrit," I replied. "Ifrits are mischievous female genies described in *Arabian Nights* who mysteriously appear, cast spells on people, and then vanish. This little terrier mysteriously appeared and cast a spell on me, like an ifrit."

I opened the crate and Ruth, who had been carrying Finn, put him in with Ifrit and shut the lid. Suddenly, all hell broke loose. The crate shook violently. Loud growling, snarling, and yipping noises filled the terminal. It sounded like a fight to the death. Passers-by stopped and stared. But as I reached to open the lid, Mrs. Veile stopped me.

"Don't worry," she advised, "They're just getting acquainted."

Thus, I had my first lesson in the social behavior of Jack Russell terriers. Like soldiers of the old Prussian Army conducting war games, Jack

Russells play with live ammunition. They sound and look like they're killing each other. It takes an expert like Mrs. Veile to know when they're not.

* * * * *

"Getting acquainted" continued after I boarded the plane and slipped the pups' crate beneath the seat in front. Heads turned, airline attendants began whispering to each other. The acoustics in the confined space of the cabin magnified the noise.

"What's in the box?" asked the lady in he seat next to me.

"Two terriers," I replied.

"You'd better pull them apart," she advised. "They're killing each other."

"No," I replied, pretending to wisdom I'd acquired just a half hour earlier, "They're just getting acquainted."

"Can I see them?" she asked.

"Why not?" I replied. Once the plane was aloft, I opened the crate. By this time the tiny pups, exhausted by play, were curled together, sleeping silently. Like Yin and Yang.

The lady melted. "Can I hold one," she asked.

"Certainly," I replied, and handed her Finn. I then scooped Ifrit into my own lap. She burrowed under my jacket and into my armpit, yawned, and resumed sleeping.

Soon, the airline attendant asked if she could hold a pup. Then another passenger. Then another. As the pups were passed from one passenger to another, the cabin filled with cooing sounds and quiet lullabies. The pups had a tranquilizing effect on everyone. When the plane landed in Great Falls, Finn and Ifrit were celebrities.

* * * * *

Diana waited at the gate wearing an anxious expression. I opened the crate and Ifrit, in no hurry to see another new face, dove under her bedding and hid her eyes. But little Finn looked up at Diana brightly and seemed to say, "I promised I'd return," Diana lifted Finn with one hand and Ifrit with the other and, nuzzling them both against her cheeks, smiled silently.

But as we walked to the airport parking lot, Diana's mood changed. "Mumtazi's in real trouble," she said. "She can't last much longer and the Millegan road's still closed. The weather's so unpredictable both the Dawsons and Carliles have been urging us not to try snowmobiling out there alone. We've got to find another way."

When we reached the Telephone Booth, I called Bud, who was wintering in town.

"There's a rancher who's got a chopper to hunt coyotes," Bud suggested. "Maybe he can give you a lift."

And so, five days later—my birthday—I found myself sharing a helicopter, looking for coyotes.

* * * * *

"None down there," the rancher said as the chopper climbed out of the Two Creeks canyon, "Let's drop Chase off then take another pass by Castle."

The chopper settled to the ground in front of the Bath House. Clouds of snow, stirred by the blades, swirled around us as I hopped out, praying for Mumtazi. Before I had reached the door, the chopper lifted off and was gone.

Mumtazi jumped into my arms when I opened the door. Although terribly thin, she otherwise seemed okay. I lay down on the floor and took her into my arms. She began to suck on my shirt and purr like a kitten. Craving love more than food, she paid no attention to the big bag of chicken I'd put down beside us. Eventually, she noticed the chicken and began to eat ravenously.

I held her in my arms for an hour then walked to the door.

"I'll be back very soon, little one," I told her. And hoped I could keep my promise.

9

Special Dogs

*There, plagued by ticks, lay Argus the hound. But suddenly aware
of Odysseus' presence, he wagged his tail and flattened his ears,
though no longer strong enough to crawl to his master. Odysseus
turned his face aside and hiding it from Eumacus wiped away a
tear . . . seeing Odysseus again in this twentieth year, the hand of
dark death seized him.*

—*Homer,*
The Odyssey, *circa 8th century B.C.*

*I would like, to begin with, to say that though parents, husbands,
children, lovers and friends are all very well, they are not dogs . . .
Once they love, they love steadily, unchangingly, till their last
breath.*

—*Elizabeth von Arnim,*
All the Dogs of My Life

Sheets of snow blew against the truck windshield as we reached the
top of Millegan Hill. A snowdrift, ten feet high, stretched across the road.
Freshly fallen snow, blown by ferocious wind, whipped across the road,
cutting through our clothes like a knife.

"Time for the snowmobiles," I said, stopping the truck. When I opened
the door, a bitter blast of wind blew it out of my hand.

"Wind-chill must be 80 below," Diana replied.

"At least it's not snowing—yet," I added. "Let's get moving before
it does."

Soon we had the snowmobiles and their sleds off the trailer. I took the
lead, pulling the sled that carried Una, Burr, and Thunderfoot. Behind
me, Diana straddled her machine which towed the sled containing Basil
and groceries. She wore her daypack backwards so that it hung on her

chest like a Snuggly, and put Finn and Ifrit in it. Finn, insisting on seeing everything, stuck his head out from underneath the cover flap. Ifrit dove headfirst to the bottom of the sack and stayed there.

We arrived at Carl and Betty Anderson's just before dark. An eerie silence hung in the air. "Ten miles to go," I said.

Carl and Betty, however, urged us to stay. "A squall's coming," Carl said, "and its nearly dark."

"The squall might last a week," I replied. "Better get a wiggle on while we can. Mumtazi can't wait much longer." So off we went.

The storm hit at dark, five miles from the ranch. Suddenly we were driving blind. Snow came in sheets and I couldn't see two feet. I knew we were on the top of the Two Creeks Hill, which had steep drop-offs on both sides. One wrong turn and we'd go over a cliff.

I looked at my feet, which was all I could see at that moment, and I noticed that the wind had blown the fresh snow clear, exposing old tire tracks. I yelled to Diana, "Follow me." We crept forward as I followed the tracks and, what seemed hours later, our front gate loomed ahead. But we weren't home yet. In our front pasture the snowmobiles, pulling heavy sleds, stalled repeatedly each time they sank into high drifts of fresh snow. After each stall we dismounted, dug out the machines with a shovel, turned around, then around again and gunned the throttle. And as soon as we got through one drift we'd meet another just ahead.

It was well after dark before we reached the ranch buildings. Diana looked down at Finn, who was still peering out from under the daypack flap.

"We're home," she said to him. "Go back down now and tell Ifrit it's safe to come out."

Drifts hard as cement and high as the roof eves surrounded the Bath House. Clammering over them we reached and opened its door. Mumtazi leaped into my arms, beside herself with joy. As I held her, purring, I don't know who was happier and more relieved.

We moved into the Manse with the dogs. Poorly insulated and never warm, this winter it carried a special chill, the indoor thermometer not rising above forty degrees. The next morning we settled in. The sun shone brightly as we dug paths between the Manse and Kitchen and Bath houses. Finn and Ifrit, happy with their new home, chased each other up and down the mountainous drifts surrounding the buildings. After breakfast, Ifrit and I left Diana in the Kitchen House with the cats and other dogs and hiked to the Hobby House, where I lit the wood stove and settled in front of my Smith Corona manual typewriter. Ifrit curled

"An unseen link, an emotional gravity too strong to resist pulls dog
and person together, and they become soul mates."

up at my feet, where she lay without moving until we returned to the Kitchen House for lunch.

And this soon became the pattern of our lives.

* * * * *

Once or perhaps twice in a lifetime, if one is lucky, one knows a dog who is very, very special. What makes a dog special? I don't know. It's mysterious. An unseen link, an emotional gravity too strong to resist pulls dog and person together, and they become soul mates. Phineas became Diana's special dog, and Ifrit mine. Each of us had never felt so close to a dog before. Yet they couldn't have been more different. While Ifrit's thick, mostly white rough coat made her resemble a mop, Finn looked remarkably like his brother, with smooth coat and similar coloration. Like Phineas, he refused to admit he was small. Both dogs were remarkable hunters with a talent for combat.

Yet the differences were equally sharp. Unlike his brother, Finn assumed he was the boss of the family. He rose to anger easily if another dog "dissed" him. He had an exaggerated sense of his own space and if another dog trespassed within it, he'd launch a mock attack on the intruder. Yet Finn also had a gentle side that Phineas lacked. Whereas the older brother remained a solemn loner, Finn was, as Aurelia Bolton had said, "a lover." Lying on your lap, he revealed that under his hard-bitten, macho exterior beat the heart of a pussycat.

By contrast, Ifrit wore sensitivity on her sleeve. Possessing an extraordinarily accurate emotional barometer, she reflected our every shift of mood. And she had what we came to call, "the loyalty gene": utter faithfulness. Having imprinted on me the moment I walked into the Hamilton Farm kennel, she never let go. Our spirits linked and we became soul mates. Intelligent beyond belief, she developed an enormous vocabulary of body language and taught herself more tricks than a magician. Her sense of play knew no bounds.

Yet despite her otherwise gentle disposition, Ifrit excelled as a hunter too. Whereas Finn took his prey head-on she conquered by patience and indirection, like a coyote. To catch gophers she simply sat up, peered over the tall grass, and waited until the rodent climbed out of its hole. Then she pounced.

So while we did not find a dog "just like" Phineas, something better happened. Finn had the good qualities of Phineas, plus some of his own. And Ifrit was a unique and precious surprise—bright, loyal, loving, and playful—perfect, we thought, in every way.

* * * * *

In June, Finn joined Diana's "team" of Dandy and the mastiffs as they explored hidden niches of the countryside—along Two Creek, the Smith, Tenderfoot, the Packdown, Gaddis, Dana Ranch, and Hound Creek Divide and Black Canyon—covering many miles a day. Ifrit never left my side, whether at work and on the range. She kept me company fishing, too, and insisted on being at my side no matter how high the water. The Smith is not a small stream, and she, having no fear of it would swim out to me even when I was wading in the middle of the river. More than once I'd rescued the little girl as she was being carried downstream by the current.

As we shared the land with these dogs, the two attachments became one. Our love for the land and love for the dogs merged. We came to enjoy the land more because we shared it with our dogs, and enjoyed the dogs more because we shared their companionship on the land. Eventually we could no more imagine riding, hiking, or fishing without Finn and Ifrit than we could imagine enjoying their company apart from these activities. And they clearly felt likewise.

This relationship animal behaviorists call, "mutualism." And according to Raymond Coppinger, professor or biology at Hampshire College and author of an important book on the behavior and evolution of dogs, it explains why dogs and humans hunt together.

"Dogs and the people are not hunting for food," he explains. Rather, we hunt because we enjoy watching the dogs and they hunt to participate with us. "The hunt is, or has become, sport."

And Finn and Ifrit's favorite sport, it would turn out, involved a furry little rodent called the hoary marmot.

* * * * *

The many rock outcroppings on Gaddis Hill above the ranch buildings were home to large populations of these rodents. Building their dens underneath or between large rocks, they ventured just far enough from these redoubts to feed on the surrounding grasses. Larger cousins of the Eastern woodchuck, they can grow to twenty pounds or more. Usually, one stands sentinel and when an intruder approaches emits a high, piercing whistle to alert the others of impending danger.

When a coyote, mountain lion, or other would-be intruder approaches, the marmots dive for cover, knowing the entrances to their mountain fortress, lying between rocks, are too small to permit invaders to enter. Feeling secure behind big boulders, they torment the enemy with whistles, which say in effect, "Ya, ya, you can't touch me!" And they were usually right—until they met Finn. For any hole they could squeeze into, he could, too.

On the first day that Finn and Ifrit, accompanying Diana on a ride, passed by the marmot enclave, the rodents let loose with their customary chorus. This not only attracted Finn, it enraged him as well. He took their taunts personally. They were "dissing" him. And he wouldn't let them get away with it!

Ifrit got excited too. And while she didn't take the marmots' taunts as personally as Finn did, her response was equally as effective. The dogs dove into the rocks after their quarry, Finn leading the way. He grabbed a surprised rodent by the nose, pulled it out, then seized the neck, and began shaking it. Meanwhile, Ifrit tugged at the other end of the animal, and within a few seconds, it was dead.

From then on, the two dogs were hooked. Marmot hunting became their favorite sport. Finn often went with Diana alone, but when Ifrit participated, the kill came more quickly. When Finn hunted marmots solo, he did not always emerge from the confrontation unscathed. The marmots got in their licks too, biting Finn about the muzzle. Before long, his face was a mass of scar tissue which he wore proudly, like a badge.

Nor were marmots Finn and Ifrit's only sport. Daily they lay waste to ground squirrel communities and took on any target of opportunity from badgers and porcupines to skunks and bears. For they were sporting dogs, not show dogs. They were bred for combat, not beauty. And this posed a dilemma: How much freedom should we give these dogs, whom we loved dearly but who insisted on courting danger?

10

Living at the Edge

An owner of a terrier worth a couple of hundred pounds is scarcely likely to run any risk with him. In an earth he may be smothered by a fall of soil or crushed by some displacement of rock; in killing the largest descriptions of vermin, foulmarts, and the like, his ears may be split and his face torn. If the scars on the latter do give an appearance of gameness, they do not enhance his beauty . . .

—*Rawdon Lee,*
The Terrier, *1889*

A dog's nervous system is in a class by itself. If it resembles anything at all, it resembles the New York Edison Company's power plant.

—*E. B. White,*
"A Boston Terrier"

At first light, I stood outside the Manse in my pajamas, barefoot in the knee-deep grass, watching a coyote carry Finn away in his teeth.

Every morning, I let Una and the Jack Russells out of the Manse. Every morning a coyote waited for them. Every morning, Una and Finn gave chase. And every morning we didn't worry because Una, being faster, would be always closest to the fleeing coyote. If the animal turned it would face Una first.

But this was not a typical morning. This time the coyote came with reinforcements. A second coyote crouched in the grass and watched as the first, followed by the two dogs, ran by. As Finn passed its hideout, the animal lunged, grabbing Finn in its teeth. The little dog screamed as the coyote shook him violently. I ran at the two, yelling. Hearing me, the coyote let go, tossing the dog about ten feet. Free at last, Finn tore toward me at top speed. The coyote, realizing his killing opportunity had passed, turned and fled.

We had discovered the flip side of Sporting Dog Heaven. Coyotes weren't the only danger. Threats lurked everywhere. Dogs could strangle in snares left by fur trappers, or consume the strychnine-laced coyote bait that probably killed Phineas. Mountain lions, species that frequently prey on dogs, abounded in the surrounding forests. Moose—especially cows protecting calves—sometimes savaged (stomped) dogs or people to death.

Almost weekly Finn or Ifrit faced a close encounter of the wild kind. Beside the confrontations with coyotes, they fell from rock ledges, had fragrant collisions with skunks, and were quilled by porcupines (whose barbed needles, left untended, work their way through the body of their victim and, if hitting a vital organ, can kill it).

And most dangerous were badgers. Among the fiercest animals for their size in the world and weighing up to thirty pounds, badgers' reputation for ferocity is legendary. "She hath very sharp teeth, and therefore is accounted a deep biting beast . . . if she be hunted abroad with hounds, she biteth them most grievously whenever she lays hold of them," wrote English sports writer Nicholas Cox in 1677.

Animals with "invincible and endless courage" was the way sports historian Henry Aiken described them in 1825. Even "two or three couple of staunch and fierce dogs will not achieve a conquest over (the badger)," Aiken wrote, "without retaining many bloody marks of his powers and of his vengeance." Along with their cousins, stoats, mink, and wolverines, they had, terrier historian Brian Plummer wrote in 1972, "an almost insane blood lust."

Yet not only were badgers abundant at the ranch, but Jack Russells were bred to hunt them. Keeping the two apart was nearly impossible. Finn and Ifrit had cornered badgers several times and averted serious injury only because I was there to pull them apart.

This behavior posed a dilemma. Finn and Ifrit loved to live on the edge, yet letting them run free put them at risk. What should we do? Russell, Serrell, and Heinemann faced similar predicaments but let their terriers hunt anyway. They did so because the dogs were bred for it and because they *admired* the dogs' courage. How could one admire their courage and not allow them to show it?

This is the dilemma sporting dogs pose. They don't make good pets. A pet is bred to be submissive and passive. Sporting dogs have has been bred to hunt. What is an asset for them—such as stamina and aggressiveness—is a liability in a pet. When not allowed opportunities to hunt they can become nervous and neurotic, driving their owners crazy. And

Diana and Finn at "The Point," Spring 1980
"Finn and Ifrit loved to live on the edge."

too often their owners respond to this behavior by putting their dog on tranquilizers, sending it to experts for submissiveness training, or, eventually, abandoning it to an animal shelter.

If we choose to adopt a sporting dog, Raymond Coppinger advises, "we should ask ourselves, what is it that I as a pet owner possess that will enhance a dog's life?" We asked ourselves this question and the answer seemed clear: We should take reasonable precautions but not restrict Finn and Ifrit's freedom. We'd have to live with the risk.

* * * * *

"Alston, wake up."

"Umm," I answered.

"Alston," Diana said again, "Ifrit's sick."

Suddenly conscious, I could hear Ifrit retching beside the bed. It was the middle of the night. I grabbed a flashlight and pointed it to the floor. There stood Ifrit, vomit around her face, looking miserable. Diarrhea covered the floor around her.

I ran to the bathhouse, returning with Kaopectate. But the diarrhea got worse. Dehydrated and shivering, she seemed near death. Putting her into the pickup, we rushed her to our vet Dr. Davis in Great Falls.

"She may have a bowel obstruction," the doctor said, as he probed her on the examining table. "They can kill quickly," he continued, adding, "We'd better open her up and take a look."

But Dr. Davis could find nothing. Ifrit's sickness had no apparent cause.

"Perhaps it's her diet," he suggested. "Let's put her on Hill's I/d prescription diet. It's easy on the digestion."

When we had returned to the ranch, Diana said, "Dr. Davis may be right. It could be Ifrit's diet. But it could also be the Manse. It's so darn cold there. The floor feels like an ice rink. Let's move into the Hobby House for the winter, where the wood stove can keep us warm."

And so we did, sleeping on the floor in sleeping bags, Finn in one with Diana, Ifrit in the other with me.

The move suited Ifrit and so did the new diet. She recovered but would never be robust. Periodically thereafter, occasional bouts of intestinal illness plagued her. Sensitive to my mood, her diarrhea returned whenever she sensed I was upset. "Nervous stomach," Dr. Davis called it. She could, he advised, succumb at any time. We couldn't take the health of this ethereal spirit for granted.

So this mysterious little genie—who seemed to have to have miraculously materialized at Hamilton Farm kennel just as I walked in the door—would remain to us a gift from God that He could just as quickly take away. A sense of urgency overcame us. Dogs find so many ways to die. Ifrit's fragility and ranch dangers meant that she or Finn might leave us without warning and without progeny. We resolved to breed them soon. If their souls weren't immortal, we thought, at least perhaps we could ensure their genes were. Not an entirely comforting kind of immortality, but better than nothing.

11

Show Dogs

Come spring, old Scott will turn up to plant his spuds . . . his spirit will linger long after he's gone. These hills would certainly never be the same without him.

—*Vernie Kitson,*
Smith River Journal, *1979*

The Greatest tragedy that can befall a breed is to become purely a fancier's dog.

—*Captain Sir Jocelyn Lucas,*
Hunt and Working Terriers, *1931*

"Jackie Bush's here," Diana called from the corral.

Standing by the horse water trough, hose in hand I could see Jackie climb out of the cab of her big, black pickup as she pulled to a stop in front of the Kitchen House.

"Hi, Jackie, what's up?" I asked as she approached.

"Have you seen Scotty Allen?" she replied. "Three weeks ago he promised to meet Mr. Custer at the mailboxes to hitch a ride to Great Falls. But he never showed up and no one's seen him since. Bud says there's no sign of him on the Smith, at either his cabin or wagon."

"Bud's right," Diana replied, joining us. "I rode by his cabin yesterday. He wasn't there."

"Must be up the Tenderfoot," Jackie said. "I'll tell Bud. He can ride up and check."

The next day Bud Dawson found Scott barely conscious, lying in the shepherd's wagon seven miles up Tenderfoot Creek. The old war veteran was too weak to walk. Bud rode back to his cabin, jumped in his Jeep Wagoneer and drove the rugged Tenderfoot Trail to Scott's wagon, where he loaded the tiny man and continued on the long and arduous Tenderfoot Trail to the Great Falls hospital.

* * * * *

Scott lingered as an invalid in Great Falls a few more years, but never returned to Millegan, thus joining the many others who left the country since we arrived in 1972.

Millegan was dwindling one person at a time. Those who hadn't yet died were gone nevertheless. No longer able to endure the harsh winters, they retired to Great Falls, Cascade, Townsend, or White Sulphur Springs, while their children, like Ted Cope and his wife, Elaine, moved to the towns too, so their children could attend school.

We were witnessing the final days of Millegan's homesteader culture—part of a concluding chapter in the decline of the pastoral way of life that had sustained humanity for millennia. Since the industrial revolution began two centuries earlier, a demographic whirlwind had swept the Western world. Displaced by poverty and machines, farmers fled to the cities. As urban centers grew, rural communities dwindled and disappeared; and the values of a new urban middle class replaced the ethic of stewardship shared by those who lived on the land.

* * * * *

Among the casualties of this whirlwind would be sporting dogs. There can be no rural sports without rural culture, and with the death of one came the transformation of the other. A new kind of dog buyer emerged, an urbanite who wanted dogs as pets and companions, not sporting comrades-in-arms.

The first visible sign of this change were dog shows, the first ever held at Newcastle-on-Tyne in England in 1859. Three years later in Birmingham, England, fox terriers competed for the first time. By the 1880s dog shows were wildly popular on both sides of the Atlantic. And as they multiplied, so did breeder associations, which set conformation standards and kept pedigree registries.

The Dandie Dinmont Association, formed in 1875, was the first for terriers, soon followed by breeder clubs for the Fox Terrier (1876), Irish Terrier (1879), Scottish Terrier and Skye Terriers (1887), Welsh Terriers (1901), Sealyham Terriers (1908), Border Terriers (1920), Kerry Blues (1922), Lakelands (1931), and the Norwich Terrier (1932). These groups, in turn, joined together to form national kennel clubs to coordinate breeder activities, promote their dogs, and organize shows. England's Kennel Club was formed in 1873 and the American Kennel Club in 1884 (the latter holding America's first show, New York's Westminster Dog Show, in 1887).

Coincidentally, the Newcastle dog show was held the same year that Charles Darwin's classic on the theory of evolution, *Origin of Species*, was published igniting an explosion of interest in breeding. All life, wrote Darwin, is governed by the law of the "survival of the fittest." Only creatures best able to adapt survived. Evolution meant progress! Hot on the heels of this doctrine came eugenics—the theory that all creatures could be "improved" through selective breeding. To show breeders, this meant that with eugenics they could produce perfect dogs.

Yet with the advent of dog shows and breed clubs came a whole new idea of what the perfect dog should be. Since sporting dogs were judged by their stamina, hunting ability, and courage, their breeders didn't care about pure pedigrees but instead regularly out-crossed to achieve the results they desired. As show dogs, by contrast, were measured by their beauty, style, and how closely they supposedly resembled their progenitors—breeders sought to produce dogs with perfect form. They wanted uniformity in appearance, and this could only be achieved by inbreeding to ensure "pure" bloodlines.

This is called, "closing the studbook": A Sealyham or Scottish terrier must have parents who are Sealyhams or Scotties, and so on back to their foundation sires, somewhere in the mists of time. And to ensure such dogs remained true to their supposed ancestral form, such show breeders often practiced what came to be known as "line breeding."

Technically, this simply signified breeding a male to a female who shared a common ancestor; but often in practice, it not infrequently became what in human terms would be called incest, such as mating a bitch to its grandfather. The purpose of line breeding was to replicate dogs, making them resemble their parents as closely as possible by reducing their genetic variability. It was, therefore, a kind of effort to ensure "genetic immortality"—to produce dogs that never changed from one generation to the next.

But rather than preventing change, line breeding accelerated it. By reinforcing familial genes it not only increased chances the pups might share desired characteristics (the same head shape or coat color, for example) but it also made more probable they'd share undesirable traits (such as the same allergy or propensity for kidney disease). And since no one knew what all the genes did, reducing their diversity put affected animals at risk in the same way that today the lack of genetic diversity threatens Cheetahs with extinction, or that declining biological diversity imperils the health of natural ecosystems.

* * * * *

While no one at the time anticipated all the ways show breeding might change dogs, nevertheless many sporting terrier people, including Reverend Russell, were horrified by this development. Russell, wrote his biographer, the Exmoor terrier man Gerald Jones (who wrote under the pen name "Dan Russell"), "regarded the show dogs with suspicion. His standard was gameness and not the perfection of the show-ring. . . . He always held that a terrier had a job of work to do and was essentially a sporting dog."

And indeed, although Reverend Russell was a founding member of the fox terrier and kennel clubs, he nonetheless was no fan of dog shows or breeder associations. He vastly preferred sporting terriers, in 1880 telling his friend, "Otter" Davies that hunt terriers are "worth their weight in gold . . . differing as much from the present show dogs as the wild Eglantine differs from the garden rose."

By 1867, just eight years after the first dog show, the famed dog expert Thomas Pearce, who wrote under the pseudonym, "Idstone" complained to the editors of *Field* magazine that "dog shows do tend to the production of useless beauties. This applies to every description of dog, and it is an evil we cannot remedy." Because dogs are judged on looks rather than ability, he noted, often prizes go to exactly the wrong dogs. "Every year," he continued, "dogs . . . will be taking first prizes, champion prizes, and medals. The drones will be decorated whilst the bees are left unnoticed . . . the test of the worth of the dog is wanting, especially as regards courage."

Consequently, Pearce noted, many purebred terriers had become "poor, craven, shivering, shy, nervous animals, destitute of any qualification for the active, hustling, neck-or-nothing life of a country gentleman's companion."

* * * * *

Subsequent sport terrier advocates shared Pearce's concern.

"Our old terriers, before the era of dog shows, were strong and healthy," wrote famed fox terrier historian Rawdon Lee in 1889.

They were not pampered as pets, as many are to-day; and they were only kept because they were muscular, hardy, and game . . . Nowadays, so long as a terrier is elegant in form, pleasant in face, and well-bred, he is worth keeping; and, however, delicate his constitution may be, should he prove good enough to win prizes, he is used at the stud, and so transmits his "blue blood" and delicacy to further generations. The former is well enough, the latter bad enough, and it is because of this carelessness in mating that so few modern terriers are as hardy.

Pearce, Lee, and their contemporaries had a right to worry. Show breeders were changing the character, conformation, and abilities of dogs as they sought to follow the fluctuations of fashion, to market their products as better pets.

Fox terriers bodies grew shorter, their legs longer, and skulls more narrow. "The better bred (fox and Sealyham terriers) are, of less value they are for work," wrote J.C. Bristow-Noble, author of *Working Terriers* in 1919. Few of the "well-bred" ones he owned were "of use for real work," he wrote, "Their noses were far from true, all grew to too large a size, particularly the Sealyhams; all lacked stamina, courage, and intelligence . . . so at length I gave up the attempt of making workers out of pedigree terriers and confined myself to building up a strain of workers from cross-bred terriers."

Jocelyn Lucas noted that "the show bench is ruining Sealyhams as a worker" and lamented the "post-war (First World War) craze for enormous heads." Cairn and West Highland terriers bred for show, Lucas reported, had become too "nervy to be a success underground," that the "show bench" has "ruined" Dandy Dinmonts, and they, along with Cairn, West Highland, and Scottish terriers are "chiefly known for show or as companions, for which latter purpose they are well suited, since they are very nice dogs, take up little room and require little exercise."

To be sure, many of those who bred dogs for show and as pets sought to avoid excessive inbreeding by matching only distantly related dogs, sometimes even importing sire and bitches from other countries. And as Lucas noted, the non-sporting dogs were nice. In fact, many made the better pets. Sporting dogs were not for everyone—even not for most people. Bred to find, chase, or kill game or varmints they were too aggressive. Many had more energy than their owners could tolerate, requiring virtual marathon runs to give them sufficient exercise to prevent their tearing the family sofa to shreds.

Jack Russells, in particular, had all these faults. What concerned sportsmen like Lucas was not that show dogs existed, but that they threatened the existence of sporting dogs. As more dogs were bred for pets and show, sporting dog numbers declined. Would, they wondered, sporting dogs—and most important, their qualities of courage, strength, stamina, and hunting ability—eventually disappear altogether?

* * * * *

Whatever its effect, nothing would contain the exploding demand for show and pet breeds. And paradoxically, the more the latter became unlike their sporting ancestors the more they would be touted as direct descendants and exact replicas of these "original" dogs.

Breed clubs began to promote theirs as "ancient"—a living relic of an earlier, pastoral time—whose blood had been kept "pure" for centuries. Their claims recalled the romance of a distant past—of shepherds attending flocks in Anatolian fields, of Borzois trotting beside troikas through the Russian steppes, of Irish Wolfhounds protecting their masters from (now extinct) Irish wolves; of Saint Bernards bringing brandy to hypothermic climbers trapped on alpine glaciers.

The American Kennel Club's *Dog Book,* also, would embrace these claims of ancient lineage for many of its dogs, including most terriers. It would tout the Fox Terrier as "an ancient breed of English origin." The Irish Terrier as "one of the oldest of the terrier breeds." The Lakeland Terrier as "one of the oldest working terrier breeds still known today." The Welsh Terrier was called "a very old breed." The Dandie Dinmont Terrier, it would tell us, was "first recorded as a distinct type of breed around 1700" (a particularly interesting claim, as this breed had been named after a fictional character by that name who appeared in Sir Walter Scott's 1815 novel, *Guy Mannering*).

Making these claims required maintaining the myth of direct descendancy from the "original" dogs. Yet such "original" dogs never existed. The very concept of a breed—meaning dogs whose reproduction was carefully restricted via a closed studbook to dogs descended from the same foundation sires—was an invention of the breeder associations. Before them, there had been no breeds in the modern sense, just types of dogs, defined not by ancestry but by function or region of origin.

However mythical, these claims of old lineage tapped the wellspring of show dogs' appeal. For while we may love our dogs whether they're deemed "ancient" or not, imagining them as relics of an early, pastoral way of life resonates within us. No matter where we live or what we do, love of the land lies in our blood. For twelve millennia, dogs and people lived on the land, working, herding, hunting, defending, rescuing. And when, beginning two hundred years ago, people began moving to cities they yearned for the pastoral way of life all the more. They still do. Dogs preserve for us an emotional connection to our bucolic past that remains in memory and imagination. And when they demand we take them for walks, they reawaken this connection. They become guides in a journey to rediscover our own genetic roots.

* * * * *

By 1900 the sport and show terrier cultures were following entirely separate paths—isolated from and hostile towards each other. Sportsmen ridiculed show dogs as inbred "freaks"; show breeders disparaged hunt terriers as uncouth mongrels. But history and demographics were on the side of the show dog. As the century wore on and the era of rural sports drew to a close, show dogs waxed as sport terriers waned.

The British public, concentrated in cities and romanticizing rather than understanding nature, turned against hunting. While it loved Wimpies and Big Macs, it didn't like killing animals. Many in the Labour Party associated the use of hunting dogs with their political opposition, the Conservatives. Militant animal-rights groups emerged, dedicated to ending all killing in the countryside, including the taking of "varmints" or nuisance animals terriers were bred to kill. Animal welfare groups opposed to hunting, such as the League Against Cruel Sports, emerged.

The British Parliament soon reflected this shift in public taste. In 1949, two Labour members of Parliament introduced bills to ban or restrict hunting. Although the bill did not pass, the Labour government then in power responded by appointing a committee to investigate all forms of hunting. And though this Committee concluded that "Fox hunting makes a very important contribution to the control of foxes . . . involves less cruelty than most other methods of controlling them (and) should therefore be allowed to continue," hunters were still not out of the woods. In 1973 Parliament passed the Badger Act, which forbade "interfering with a badger sett," and in 1978 it declared otter hunting illegal.

The authors of these laws ignored that badger numbers were rising, that there was evidence they might be spreading disease, that badger diggers often didn't kill their quarry but only relocated them, and that pollution and loss of habitat, not hunting (which took very few animals), had decimated the otter. Few seemed to anticipate that, after digging was banned, government animal control agents would be gassing badgers in great numbers. Nor, apparently, did anyone realize that, for more than a century, fox and otter hunters had proved themselves these species' best friends.

For although the government began enacting these restrictions with the best intentions—to protect wildlife—they would have the opposite effect, the same as would happen in America if the government were to ban Trout Unlimited, Ducks Unlimited, the National Wildlife Foundation, and the Boone and Crockett Club.

* * * * *

In this way, thanks to the new anti-hunting laws, declining agriculture and the growth of show breeding, sporting dogs continued to dwindle. While some bird hunters, stockmen, and others still raised dogs such as Labrador retrievers and border collies for sport or work rather than show, they had become a distinct minority.

Meanwhile, paradoxically, in England JRs were becoming widely popular. Even as they remained a favorite with foxhunters, the working classes also had discovered the little terrier, making it a pet or putting it to work killing rats, stoats, and rabbits. The new owners began breeding it for such a variety of jobs that "the mongrelly Jack Russell," as terrier historian Brian Plummer put it, "became even more mongrelly."

"The first hunt terrier shows I attended in the 1950s," Plummer wrote, "were indeed extraordinary sights, with the most amazingly variable types of dog being proudly shown as genuine Jack Russells; some of them displayed hints of collie, or, not infrequently, dachshund, in their lineage. Many were quite hideous, but handsome is as handsome does, and some of those monstrosities proved to be incredibly good workers."

Nevertheless, the mongrelly aspect of Jack Russells troubled many owners because they could not say what a Jack Russell was and feared their favored dog was losing its identity. To counter this mongrelly drift, in 1974 those so concerned formed the Jack Russell Terrier Club of Great Britain, appointing Plummer its first chairman. Its first task was to define the breed and set conformation standards. And the result was chaos.

"Near-riot prevailed" at those early meetings, Plummer later recalled. Nevertheless, they did set a "standard of sorts." At the beginning, Plummer wrote, "any dog that conformed to a rough description of a Jack Russell terrier was eligible for registration in the initial register." And not surprisingly, the differences between these dogs were so huge that by 1980 many members urged they close the studbook. And this was, Plummer reports, a mistake.

"To be brutally frank," he wrote, "many Jack Russell strains could well benefit from using the blood of other breeds." But his opinion would not prevail. Soon after, some club leaders would approach England's Kennel Club to have their dogs recognized as a distinct breed.

* * * * *

Thus, many English Jack Russells began to succumb to the inexorable trend towards breed standards and the closed studbook, thereby following the paw prints of many Scotties, Sealyhams, Dandie Dinmonts, and other sporting terriers.

In America at this time, however—the same period that Phineas, Finn, and Ifrit had joined our family—the JR still seemed immune from this trend. Unlike the English Jack Russell, which was already popular, its American counterpart remained virtually unknown outside foxhunting communities. Ailsa Crawford's Jack Russell Terrier Club of America, still emphasizing performance over pedigree, refused to close the studbook completely or set narrow conformation standards or join the American Kennel Club. Instead, the little dog soldiered on as a "glorified mongrel."

But how long could it hold out?

We didn't even know to ask. Isolated in our wilderness cocoon, we remained unaware of the breed controversies swirling elsewhere. But before long, we'd discover we didn't live in a cocoon at all, but in a microcosm, where Millegan's decline and our dogs' fate would enact, on a small stage, the story of land and dogs everywhere.

12

Leaving Millegan

Stover farewell! Still fancy's hand shall trace
Thy pleasure's past in all their former grace,
And I will wear and cherish, though we part,
Thy dear remembrance ever at my heart.

> *—Penned by Reverend Russell's friend,*
> *George Templer in 1825 after losing his*
> *beloved estate, Stover, through bankruptcy.*

Asiatic poetry had created the hero Yudhishtira, who refused
to enter heaven at all unless his dog might accompany him.

> *—John Lockwood Kipling,*
> Beast and Man in India, *1904*

Basil and I sat with Finn and Ifrit at the top of the embankment above the Smith River flood plain enjoying the warm spring sun. A hundred feet below us, I could see a sow bear with two black and one cinnamon yearling cubs quietly grazing the rich, spring grass. The dogs, whose view was obscured by intervening willows, could not. So we rested together quietly as I continued to watch the munching bears. Then suddenly Basil saw them too and took off like a shot, quickly followed by the JRs.

The dogs were on the bears in an instant, colliding out of my sight behind the willows. But while I couldn't see the encounter, I heard it. The almost human cry of the sow pierced the air, followed by sounds of a tussle. Then suddenly the sow and two cubs burst through the bushes in front of me, running hard uphill, followed closely by Basil and the Jack Russells. And just as I was beginning to wonder what had happened to

Diana, Finn, Basil, Ifrit, Alston, and Una

"It was a moment to savor, this Spring of 1981—for the dreaded time was approaching when we would have to leave the ranch."

baby bear number three, the furry cub burst through the bushes, running behind the dogs and seeming to cry, "Hey, wait for me!"

The dogs returned a minute later, tongues hanging out, looking happy and pleased with themselves.

It was a moment to savor, this April of 1981—for the dreaded time was approaching when we would have to leave the ranch.

It had been a tough winter. Our first breeding of Finn and Ifrit the previous summer failed to produce pups. *Group Memory* appeared in September and promptly bombed. A week later Una got sick. Just before we were to leave on the book promotion tour, her hind legs collapsed. When we lifted her up, she'd take a few steps then fall back on her haunches again. We left her with Dr. Davis on our way to the airport. But he couldn't save her. Conferring with him a week later by phone from Minnesota we agreed to put her to sleep.

For five years she had been our only dog, our soul mate and company in isolation. My hike with her and Phineas that day in 1977 on the Dana Ranch remained a priceless memory. Her company alone, during the depths of our debt, lifted our spirits.

"Eight years is all she had," Diana said. "She was cheated."

"Eight years is all we had with her," I replied. "We were all cheated."

* * * * *

Winter had come early and refused to leave. By February, we were still waiting in vain for a thaw. The Atlantic Monthly Press signed me to write another book which I would call *Playing God in Yellowstone*, but offered an advance so small it was gone in three months. With nothing else to make ends meet, we arranged a second mortgage line of credit with the Federal Land Bank,

"Alston, we're going broke," Diana blurted as we sat by the wood stove watching the snow fall outside the Kitchen House window.

"We're always going broke," I replied, as Ifrit jumped into my lap. "I'm not afraid of going broke. I'm afraid of being broke. And if we're lucky that won't happen until the day after we die."

"Be serious," Diana admonished. "We can't go on like this."

"Maybe *Playing God* will be a best-seller," I said hopefully.

"Perhaps," she said, eying me skeptically as she stroked Finn's ears. "But what do we eat in the meantime?"

"I'll think of something," I said.

But I couldn't. By April we were just deeper in debt.

* * * * *

Diana and I sat quietly in the horse pasture, warming ourselves in the sun and watching a pair of Bobcats catch ground squirrels to feed their kittens. When one caught a gopher, it carried the rodent's body to the base of the large Douglas fir at the upper edge of the meadow. When the cats had accumulated several carcasses each, they put them in their mouths and headed up the mountain to feed their young.

Each spring for several years, Diana and I had sat like this, on the grass in spring watching the cats repeat their hunting ritual. This time, speaking what was on both our minds Diana asked, "How can we keep the ranch?" I remained silent for a moment as we watched the cats disappear up the coulee. "I could always get a job," I replied, finally, "but then we couldn't live here. And if we stay on, we'll go broke."

"In other words," she said, "The only way to keep the ranch is to leave it and the only way to stay on the ranch is to lose it. But Alston, we just can't leave. For nine years that one thought kept us going. We promised ourselves that no matter what we'd stay here until we died. We've not just planted deep roots here—we've buried souls here. We can't abandon them."

"We could put the place on the market and ask an outrageously high price for it," I suggested. "And if we're lucky, it might be years before we received an offer. In the meantime we could continue to live off the line of credit."

But the plan didn't work. In early May we listed the ranch with a real estate agent and almost immediately received an offer for the asking price. It caught us completely by surprise. Until that moment, we had continued to hope. Somehow, something would come along, we told ourselves, and we wouldn't have to sell. However irrational, we continued to believe we'd live at the Ben Dunn place forever. Now suddenly we had to leave, and soon. The buyers wanted us gone by July.

* * * * *

Mumtazi died in May. Like Una, her hindquarters collapsed. Dr. Davis couldn't say why. She walked up to me dragging her hind legs on the ground, a feline paraplegic too weak to jump in my lap. I picked her up, held her close and let her knead my chest and suckle my shirt. She'd been with us for sixteen years and what we'd been through together had forged an unbreakable bond. But her time had come. Dr. Davis put her to sleep. We buried her under the Douglas fir in the horse pasture, but the next day found her grave empty. An animal—probably a skunk—had taken it away.

A week later Basil inexplicitly attacked our newborn colt, a dun named Ben Dunn, and would have killed it had I not intervened. Unable to trust the dog around horses again we took him to Dr. Davis, who found him a good home at a neighboring ranch. Like all Mastiffs we'd known before, Basil had been a sweet, gentle dog. What triggered his attack? We would never know. But not long after leaving us, he would die of a brain aneurism, leaving us to wonder if there had been a connection.

Then the rains came. It rained, and rained, and rained. More rain fell during the last two weeks of May than during many entire years. Water poured off Gaddis Hill and down the coulees in torrents, loosening a deafening roar heard for miles. A thousand foot waterfall swept down Suicide Trail toppling old growth pines and firs and carrying mountains of debris into the river. The Smith swelled until it covered the entire flood plain from one canyon wall to the other, forming a half mile-wide caldron that raced with ferocious impatience to its rendezvous with the Missouri.

When the flood subsided, the river was unrecognizable. The pool where our boys swam had disappeared—filled by silt. Shallow gravel bars obliterated the spots that once held big trout. Gone, too, were the swirling pools of emerald green water that lay in the shadow of the cliffs. The lovely Tenderfoot became a naked ditch, devoid of meanders and vegetation, as though it had been bulldozed. No grass, willows, or cottonwoods grew along its banks. If humans had done this damage, they'd have been arrested for committing an environmental crime. But humans didn't do it.

"Perhaps," Diana said, "This is God's way of saying it's time to leave."

* * * * *

I sat with Ifrit on a boulder at the river's edge, the two of us alone in the canyon, I tying a fly as the July sun warmed our backs. Suddenly Finn appeared, moving with his easy rocking-horse canter and greeting us with delight. Behind him appeared Diana on Dandy. In this mere speck of time, I caught another glimpse of eternity, a crystalline image that would remain forever bright in memory.

The next day we packed our remaining belongings in a U-Haul truck and said goodbye to Millegan, leaving behind the spirits of those we had loved there— Ravelin, Antinomy, Phineas, Little Orphan Annie, Zoomie, Una, Mumtazi, Basil.

We moved to Paradise Valley, 125 miles to the south. On the first day there, Thunderfoot disappeared. We looked for him everywhere, combed the neighborhood, put ads in the local paper, and checked with the animal shelter but never found him. Soon Burr began to grieve for his friend. Within a month, he was dead of leukemia.

The animals we love frame our lives. Their arrival into the family as pups, kittens, or foals signals a joyous new beginning and their death marks the end of one period and the beginning of another. In Millegan, the land and animals we loved had fused in our hearts. Now only Finn, Ifrit, and fragments of memory remained. A chapter of our lives had ended and a new one was about to begin.

13

Paradise

Who's this—alone with stone and sky?
It's only my old dog and I—
It's only him; it's only me;
Alone with stone and grass and tree.

—Siegfried Sassoon,
"Man and Dog"

Dogs are like Emmanuel Kant, who always
wanted to take the same walk.
The less it changes, the happier they are.

—Roger Grenier,
The Difficulty of Being a Dog

The waters of the Yellowstone River begin their long journey to the sea as melt from a permanent ice field on the slopes of 12,156-foot Younts Peak in Wyoming's Absaroka Mountains. They pick up volume as they race through the Teton Wilderness and down Yellowstone Park's majestic Thorofare Valley, before emptying into Yellowstone Lake. On leaving the lake, they carve a magnificent gorge known as the Grand Canyon of the Yellowstone. Then, on entering Montana, they pass through a swift and dangerous funnel known as Yankee Jim Canyon before proceeding down a long, broad valley fed by small streams pouring from surrounding mountains. The valley's name is "Paradise."

After leaving Millegan we built our home here, on a dead-end road on the side of the mountains. I resumed work on *Playing God* and Diana began to write a novel. With Finn and Ifrit as companions, we explored our new surroundings.

Behind our house, a trail entered the Absaroka-Beartooth Wilderness. We hiked up and around it virtually every day. Usually I went alone after work with Finn and Ifrit; but sometimes Diana, riding Dandy, joined us on what we called, "walk-rides." Often we "bushwhacked" off the trail altogether, taking detours to the broad, grassy foothills and copses of aspen and cottonwood that lined the edge of the mountain forests. Over time, we came to know every rock and tree; and with this familiarity, our treks grew more precious. We savored the small things: the dampness of spring, the wild flowers of summer, the dark shadows of fall, and the solitude of winter. The hikes and walk-rides with the dogs became the high point of our days.

Occasionally, we followed the path as it climbed thousands of feet, where we picnicked in a high alpine meadow surrounded by barren peaks. Together, we sometimes scaled them—I scrambling hand over hand up cliffs, passing the dogs up to a higher ledge before climbing up myself. And at least once every year in September, around Diana's birthday, we continued up to the barren, windy pass next to a permanent ice field that seemed to scrape the sky.

Yet here, in Paradise too, Finn and Ifrit found a way to live at the edge—challenging moose, badgers, coyotes, and foxes and treading in territory heavily populated with mountain lions. Prompted by these reminders of their mortality, in May 1982 we tried again to breed them.

* * * * *

One day the following July I sat on the couch in my study with Ifrit in my lap. Restless and panting, she shifted positions but couldn't get comfortable. Diana asked, "Is this it?" I didn't know. Neither of us knew. The sum-total of our whelping experience had been watching our little hampster, Rufus, produce a throng of little pink babies. And until then we'd thought Rufus a boy. Later we'd learn how to help Ifrit. But we didn't know then.

Ifrit's labor continued but nothing happened. Then a small gray dime-sized spot appeared at her bottom—the amniotic sac. We waited. The sac grew to the size of a quarter then bulged outward. We waited some more. It emerged, sticking out two inches.

Then it stopped. Ifrit strained but nothing happened. We later learned we could have helped her by using a drug to stimulate contractions, or by putting a soft towel around the sac and gently pulling it out. But we didn't know that then. We just waited.

With a final heave, Ifrit expelled the sac. In it was the loveliest little male pup we've ever seen, with beautiful black, brown, and white mark-

Sid and Nobie, August 1982
"The second pup came quickly."

ings. Exactly like Phineas. But he was dead. He had been stuck in the birth canal too long and it had pinched off the umbilical cord, blocking the blood supply.

The second and last pup came quickly—not as pretty as the first, but still lovely, a gift nonetheless. The English poet, William Blake, called God,"Nobodaddy." We decided to call the pup, "Nobodoggy," "Nobie" for short.

* * * * *

Every once in a while you meet dogs with so many quirks they drive you crazy. Some drink out of the toilet bowl; others chew slippers or howl like hyenas at the sound of thunder. So, too, Nobie was a bundle of exasperating eccentricities. A rough-coated, short-legged little dog with pretty brown markings, chock full of anxieties. Perhaps it was birth trauma—waiting so long in the uterus. Perhaps it was Finn, who gruffly rejected his son whenever the pup approached him. And it certainly was, at least in part, his being the only surviving pup. Having littermates during the first eight weeks of life, canine behaviorists tell us, is critically important to the development of a pup's personality. It teaches him to interact with other dogs; to develop self-confidence through competition for the mother's milk; and, through enjoying the feelings of warmth and security by snuggling with his siblings, to teach him how to relax.

Poor Nobie had none of these benefits. Besides us, only Ifrit showed him love. He was the apple of her eye. Every morning, every day, she washed his face as if to say, "I love you." But even this wasn't enough.

As Nobie grew up, his personality developed more kinks than a corkscrew. And having so many vulnerabilities made us love him all the more. Always lonely, he was afraid of his shadow. Extremely sensitive, he needed special love and understanding. He feared Finn, thunder, lightning, darkness, leaving the house, and entering it. In mornings, he refused to leave his crate. When outdoors, he wouldn't come in. He suffered from panic attacks, sometimes triggered by thunder but often for no apparent reason. When they hit him during a hike, he dove under the nearest bush and hid for hours, on occasions an entire day.

Once he disappeared while accompanying Diana and Dandy on a ride. She searched for him for hours without success. That night we lay in bed listening to the coyotes howl up on the meadow where Diana had lost him and wondered if we'd ever see him again. The next day Diana and

"As Nobie grew up, his personality developed
more kinks than a corkscrew."

Dandy retraced their steps. Near a copse of willows, the horse startled, pricked his ears, and stared at the bushes. Riding closer, Diana saw Nobie peering at her through the leaves like a little fox.

The next time he disappeared on a cold February day. He and I had hiked through deep snow to a ridge above our house when he vanished. After hunting fruitlessly for him until dark, I went home. When the next morning I returned to the ridge he was there to greet me, standing on a rock wagging his tail joyously. From then on, we called the spot "Nobie's Rock."

Thus, did Nobie join our little troop, alternately bringing laughter and tears. And soon he had sisters.

* * * * *

Once again I sat on the couch, Ifrit laboring in my lap, panting—another hard delivery.

"We can't risk a pup dying like last time," Diana said. "Let's take her to the vet right now."

I jumped behind the wheel of our Subaru station wagon, with Diana sitting on the seat behind me, and Ifrit lying on a pad in the cargo area. We sped over the Bozeman Pass. Suddenly Diana said, "a pup's coming."

Looking in my rear view mirror, I saw Diana turn around in her seat. "A beautiful little girl," she said, then a moment later, "and another!" We continued to the vet's, who declared mother and pups okay. Two females. One, lovely brown and white face with black rings around her eyes, we would call, "Panda." The other, identical to Ifrit—almost entirely white with just a little brown around one ear and the opposite side eye—we named, "Little Nell."

Both pups grew to be gentle, short-legged rough-coats. Panda would go through life with innocent bewilderment. Little Nell inherited Ifrit's magical capacity for love and play, and would soon be teaching herself tricks and games.

I liked Panda but adored Nell. But when they were eight weeks, Diana's oldest friend and former college roommate, Laurie Archer, came to visit and fell for Nell as well. We couldn't deny Laurie. So she took Nell home with her to Santa Fe, changing her name to Dasher.

Thus, it was Panda who stayed with our family. In her, we at last had, we thought, the seeds to ensure—not through line breeding but rather by mating her to an unrelated male—that a fraction of Finn and Ifrit's genes would survive them. And although just a small kind of immortality, it was better than none at all.

Alston holding Panda (left) and Nell, September 1984
"'A beautiful little girl,' she said, then a moment later, 'and another!'"

"Ifrit became my muse."

Panda joined my hikes and became Diana's stalwart companion on rides. Over her life this little "energizer bunny " as we sometimes called her, although barely ten inches tall, would cover more ground than any dog we'd ever had, before or since. Inheriting Finn's easy, rocking-horse gait she never tired. An uncomplaining little trooper, always there and seldom noticed, she evinced a stoicism that would make us love and admire her increasingly throughout her life.

* * * * *

With the addition of Nobie and Panda, our little flock of Jack Russells, now numbering four, settled into the gentle rhythms of the writer's life.

Ifrit became my muse. With her, I couldn't possibly feel lonely in my study. Nor, since Nobie and Panda were usually there as well, could I feel bored, as I was too distracted watching them play keep-away with my fountain pen.

And it was Ifrit who set my schedule. She decided when I'd worked long enough and that it was time for a hike, announcing her decision by jumping into my lap and rushing to the door. And if a telephone call or another distraction interrupted this routine, she went berserk, barking, dashing about like a demon, and threatening mayhem if I didn't get out of the house immediately.

* * * * *

In this way Ifrit and her family encouraged a regular life that balanced walking with contemplation—a role that suited them just fine because, unlike humans who, being restless novelty-seekers lack wisdom, they understood the value of routine for themselves as well as for people.

From time to time throughout the 1980s, other dogs joined our troop as well. Among these were several giant dogs we adopted to replace Una and Basil as bodyguards for the terriers. But all suffered debilitating genetic defects. We adored Willow, a gentle Mastiff, but before she was two years old she succumbed to kidney disease. We replaced her with another Mastiff named "Annie" who soon turned vicious—twice attacking and nearly killing Finn—and had to be put to sleep.

Clearly, a century's inbreeding had taken its toll on large breeds. Of the six giants we'd had who were not killed by cars, only Una lived beyond four. The Mastiff in particular, a once lovely dog, had clearly inherited severe problems. We began to wonder: are Jack Russells safe?

14

America Discovers Jack Russells

It looks as if the Jack Russell is in great danger of becoming a kennel club registered breed and whatever safeguards may be taken, once that happens they will, in no time, end up as a very smart, very popular, very expensive and in many cases, very useless terrier.

—David Harcombe,
Badger Digging with Terriers, *1985*

In 1981, America discovered Jack Russells. Hitherto known only in foxhunting communities, they would become famous throughout the country. Signaling this transformation was an article published in *Sports Illustrated* in October that year entitled, "The Mutt with a Touch of Class." Historically accurate, it celebrated the terrier's mixed breeding and sporting ancestry and its phenomenal courage, strength, and feisty nature. It explained that the Jack Russell is a "mongrelly dog," not bred for conformation and American Kennel Club (AKC) dog shows but rather often out-crossed for sport.

"Jack Russell people," the magazine wrote,

> . . . are not interested in dog shows. They are interested in a working terrier, one that will dig to foxes and dislocate the spines of rats, while at the same time making a fine house pet. The knock against the AKC is that as soon as a breed achieves recognition, it is shown in prestigious events like the Westminster. As soon as it is shown, there are champions. As soon as there are champions, there are champions that are too valuable to 'go to ground.' The working qualities of the breed become secondary to physical conformation and 10 generations later you have a lovely looking terrier that will flee before *Rattus norwegicus*.

Sports Illustrated concluded presciently, "the one thing this hardy animal probably couldn't survive is acceptance by the masses." But mass acceptance lay just around the corner. During the 1980s, in both England and America, the popularity of the little terrier grew enormously; and as it did yet more Jack Russell breeding clubs appeared, each dedicated to preserving its version of the "original" dog.

This, however, was all Jack Russell breeders agreed on. On everything else they squabbled with terrier-like ferocity.

As it had been in the 1970s, the question still at issue was: What is a Jack Russell? Is it a "purebred" with a pedigree proving it descended from Reverend Russell's own pack, or is it merely any terrier that can do the job he intended? Should all JRs resemble the Parson's dogs? And what was that conformation? Were "original" Jack Russells short or tall, thin or thick, rough or smooth? Battle lines were drawn. Competing clubs touted different versions of the "traditional" dogs.

In 1984, ten years after Brian Plummer helped organize the Jack Russell Club of Great Britain, others founded a competing association that would later be called the Parson Russell Terrier Club. Alarmed about what their web site later described as "a scheme [by others] to promote the smaller terrier as the Jack Russell" and fearing that "the original type of terrier would die out or simply be regarded as a mongrel," they dedicated themselves to preserving the "older, true, distinctive type" they believed still "persisted . . . in the West Country [of England]."

Calling their dog the "Parson Russell Terrier," to distinguish it from the "abundance of cross-breed hunt terriers, indiscriminate in size referred to as Jack Russells," the Club closed the studbook and drew up a standard, stipulating the "ideal height" to be around fourteen inches.

* * * * *

Unfortunately, closing the studbook inevitably leads to what biologist Raymond Coppinger would later call, "an evolutionary dead-end":

> Sexual isolation from the greater population of dogs leads almost inevitably to dire consequences for those dogs that get trapped in a pure breed. . . . Once the stud book is closed on a breed, it is unbelievable how fast they become inbred . . . They are caught in a genetic trap.

Here was the paradox of line breeding: intended as a way to preserve the original dogs, it accelerated their transformation by reinforcing undesirable traits, including genetically transmitted diseases. Yet despite its risks, the movement to close the studbook and promote the leggier variety of JRs as the "original" type soon crossed the pond.

In 1985, some American breeders founded the Jack Russell Terrier Breeders Association, which would eventually become the Parson Russell Terrier Association of America (PRTAA) to promote "breeding, working and continuance of the purebred, traditional Parson Russell Terrier."

Established "in response to growing concerns that the breed was being misrepresented as a short-legged terrier," the PRTAA set forth detailed standards which covered everything from "expression" ("keen, direct, full of life and intelligence") to shape ("the height at withers is slightly greater than the distance from the withers to tail"). No dogs under twelve inches were allowed (fourteen inches "ideal"); coat must be "broken or smooth" (apparently no rough coats). The personality of the Parson Russell, it declared, is "bold though cautious." And while "submissiveness is not a fault," being "quarrelsome" is. "Overt aggression towards another dog" is a disqualification.

* * * * *

Traditional sporting JR people could hardly believe how anyone could conceive these standards, for they disregarded so much they knew about the dog. By stipulating taller terriers, the PRTAA ignored "Otter" Davies description of Reverend Russell's Trump as "being the size of a vixen fox"—i.e., around thirteen inches and longer than tall, as well as Alys Serrell's advice that a JR "should not be much over fourteen inches . . . a size even smaller than this is better . . . a leggy dog is of little or no use for underground work."

Sometimes referring to these leggy "Parson Russells" as "spiders," these critics hoped they were just a fad that would soon disappear.

"There are many good Jack Russells about, whatever their makeup," English sporting dog writer David Harcombe wrote in 1985. "Smooth or rough coated, short or long legged, take your pick, though the short-legged are not so popular at the moment. However, they will return to popularity once people realize their advantage over the 'spiders.'"

But Harcombe and the other critics had been mistaken. The show "Parson Russell" was here to stay and the mythologizing of its past just begun. Breed club founders, however well intentioned, succumbed to the illusion that infects so many in the dog business—to tout their dog as "original" and "pure." But the Jack Russell was never a breed, never "pure," and never fit any conformation standard, as those who had long known the dog were quick to point out.

"From time to time," wrote Brian Plummer, "one sees advertisements for 'genuine' Jack Russell terriers, always descended from Jack Russell's dogs . . . The reader would do well always to treat such claims with a pinch of salt—I recommend a block or two." The reasons to be skeptical, he explained, were that "the original bloodline would have become highly diluted by outcrosses with other strains (and) few working-terrier breeders keep anything like accurate pedigrees."

"After some ninety years," Gerald Jones, who knew Heinemann, wrote in 1979, "there can be none of the original Russell blood left today. Even if one could trace a terrier's pedigree back to Russell's dogs, there must have been so many out-crosses that the original blood would have been thinned to the vanishing point. If one had bred true, one would now be producing half-wits."

Certainly, none who knew Russell, Heinemann, or Serrell believed any such thing as a "pure" or "original" Jack Russell ever existed. As Lord Paltimore (whose father and grandfather had been close friends of Russell) explained to Lucas, "It is entirely misleading to talk of a 'Jack Russell' terrier. Mr. Russell always said that he had *no special strain* of terrier. If he saw a likely dog he would acquire it, and if suitable in his work he would breed from it, but he never kept any special strain."

In 1930, Lucas related how Heinemann, whom he knew personally, "bore witness to the fact that the sporting parson bought any terrier of the stamp he liked that would go to ground," and that G. P. Williams, a Master of the Four Burrows Hunt in Cornwall, told him that Russell visited his grandfather every year "and took any draft terrier that he gave him."

* * * * *

Russell and his successors, also, had worried that show breeding might undermine not only their terrier's sporting conformation, but its fighting spirit as well. Although they didn't favor dogs with too "hard" a mouth, they nevertheless bred them for courage and aggression. And the PRTAA's tolerance of, or preference for, a "cautious" and "submissive" dog would have been inconceivable to them.

Alys Serrell wouldn't keep three terriers together in a pen lest two kill the third. But she didn't consider this a fault. She recognized that such quarrelsomeness was a necessary trait of any small dog bred to challenge a fox or badger. Likewise, Lucas noted that "some terriers fight like demons." But he didn't suggest this a flaw, but rather an indication that dealing with fights was a JR owner's lot. "If two terriers have a set-to and there happens to be a stable door, a wall, a fence or a gate handy," he wrote, "take them and hang them over it, one on each side. They will soon let go, and you can then put them on leads. It is a simple and efficient way and saves further bites."

Those who might consider feistiness a fault or cautiousness a virtue should consider the description by Major John Bell Irving in 1931 of a pack of hard-bitten, otter-hunting terriers as they are released from a van in preparation for a hunt. And although the dogs he describes are Border terriers, they could just as well have been Jack Russells:

Terrific screeching, yapping and snarling sounds are heard, and a number of little red and black-and-tan animals are seen fighting desperately to get to the surface, and as near the outlet as possible. These are the terriers . . . a queer-looking lot of seven hard-bitten, wiry little devils. Queer-looking, chiefly because of the scars, which have not improved their beauty.

Firstly, there is black "Sandy" a heavy-coated, little grizzled black and tan fellow, with a pointed face (because half one side of his mouth is not there! Likewise half his nose) and he is none too true a mover behind, caused by a shaking from hounds in his younger days. Old "Sandy" is rated to be the hardest thing in these parts that ever faced anything with teeth and claws. . . .

Then there is old "Dinger." . . . a serious-looking, old, hard case, with a grey face...he, like 'Sandy' is disfigured, and amongst other things has a broken nose, through which he snuffles. . . .

. . . then there is old "Bess," not really old in years, but very battered. She has no teeth to speak of on one side, and her tongue hangs out, giving her a very comic appearance. "Bess" never fails, and, being small, can get into anything.

"Darkie" . . . has an everlasting snarl on his countenance, having had a large snick taken out of his upper lip by the first otter he ever met. There is nothing "Darkie" won't tackle.

. . . lastly comes "Nailer," a little, very bright red dog. You can't defeat "Nailer." He will go anywhere, and tackle anything, and is always on the spot.

There are one or two familiar faces not out to-day, among these being "Siki" and "Jeff" both sons of "Tinker," and both under repair. . . . having got "chewed up" their last time out.

* * * * *

Although the breed clubs' depiction of the "Parson Russell" rested more on myth than historical fact, the image they created—of the dog as gentle, purebred, and leggy—continued to build. And as it did, those who preferred shorter dogs established their own clubs, declaring "shorties" as the true JR, and naming their's the "Russell Terrier" to distinguish it from the "Jack Russell" (i.e., all sizes) and "Parson Russell" (the leggy variety).

Whereas before the advent of breed clubs JRs carried such a wide variety of genes that often dogs in the same litter differed widely in shape, size, and coat, soon narrowly-bred uniformity would be the rule. "Russell terrier" advocates bred only short dogs and "Parson Russell Terrier" supporters produced only the taller variety. As both had closed their studbooks, tall and short JRs were well on their way to becoming separate breeds.

The splintering continued. Some breeders specialized in rough coats, others in smooth coats, while still others catered to customers who wanted terriers with lots of color. JR breeder associations divided and multiplied, specializing in dogs conforming to ever more narrow and rigid standards. The genetic world of JRs was shattered into countless shards, each piece a genetic dead-end. Soon, the show circuit and kennel club recognition would accelerate this inbreeding as show champions (so-called, "matadors") fathered an ever-increasing percentage of newborns.

* * * * *

Meanwhile, in England anti-hunting bias continued to build, further threatening the Jack Russell. By 1980 an anti-foxhunting animal rights group, the Hunt Saboteurs, founded in the 1960s, began capturing national attention with direct-action (sabotage) and public protests. Sending busloads of activists to the countryside to harass foxhunters, it began swaying national sentiment towards an absolutist view of animal rights. Influenced by this shift, both political parties established "compassion" platforms.

The same trend in public values influenced many JR fanciers. In 1980 one English JR breed club member, the author Mona Huxham, apparently unaware that the UK government was concerned that badgers were spreading tuberculosis to cattle and had already decided to begin culling them, remarked approvingly that "thankfully, a bill protecting the badger was passed by parliament at the end of 1973."

The ironies were inescapable: fanciers loved a dog that had been created by cross-breeding, but banned the practice from their own ranks. The public revered the "hunting-parson" Russell, but not hunting. It loved the dog that rural sports had created, but turned against the rural sports that would sustain him.

"Prepare the chains and manacles," David Harcombe observed in 1985:

> In the world of field sports one particular character is the social outcast of the day. Reviled and hated by the anti "blood sport" brigade . . . it has become more fashionable to "hound" him [the terrier] than the fox! . . . It is one of the wonders of the age that he survived so long. Indeed, it is fair to say that he is now almost extinct, unlike the badger, which thrives as never before.

15

Seaching for "Genetic Immortality"

I would have no pleasure living in a world where dogs did not exist.

—Arthur Schopenhauer

The genes are immortal . . . We, the individual survival machines of the world, can expect to live a few more decades. But these genes of the world have an expectation of life that must be measured not in decades but in thousands and millions of years.

—Richard Dawkins,
The Selfish Gene

The macrocosm had begun to swallow the microcosm.

By the mid-1980s our cocoon had been breached and the ongoing transformation of Jack Russells into "Parson Russells" began to intrude into our little world as well. While Harcombe and others worried about the future of sporting terriers, we found ourselves concerned about the future of our own sporting terriers. We began to fear that, not only might Finn and Ifrit's little family die out, but also that sporting Jack Russells might disappear altogether. Then we'd be left with no terriers to take their place.

* * * * *

We first began to worry after my book, *Playing God in Yellowstone*, appeared in 1986. A cautionary tale, it revealed how the park's land, vegetation, and wildlife declined once the region's first land stewards, the Native Americans, had been forced to leave and its new tenants, the National Park Service, neglected to follow Indian stewardship practices.

Before Europeans arrived, Indians had cared for the land through burning forests and grasslands to increase wildlife habitat and through hunting, which prevented one species, such as the elk, from growing overly abundant and destroying the habitat of others. But Yellowstone rangers didn't follow the Indians' example. Instead, they followed Park Service policy that stipulated the best way to keep the park in "original condition" was to let "nature takes its course" and do nothing at all. The result of this benign neglect was ecological disaster.

Because rangers didn't burn the forests, the palatable plants that usually sprout after fires disappeared, thereby depriving wildlife of important food sources. Because they didn't cull game herds, elk and bison numbers grew tenfold. These overly-abundant animal populations, having run out of food, ate the vegetation that protected river banks from erosion and which fed many other species—including beaver, black and grizzly bears, mule and white-tail deer, antelope, and mountain sheep. Critical wildlife species dwindled and soil erosion accelerated.

Thus, the story of Yellowstone paralleled those of Devon, Millegan, and other lightly populated areas, revealing once again how bad things happen to the land when agrarian communities die. Though praised by ecologists, *Playing God* proved controversial with the media, and its publication changed our lives abruptly. I took frequent trips for interviews and lectures, joined the mastheads of magazines and traveled constantly. I started a new book that would require still more trips for research.

These demands kept me away from the dogs. Even when home I was often too busy to hike. Ifrit suffered most. When I was home she stuck to me like glue. And when I prepared to leave on a trip she trembled, vomited, and suffered attacks of diarrhea. After I left, Diana couldn't console her.

As our hikes became less frequent they grew more precious. A silent intimacy prevailed on these treks, as I savored their company and sensed our time together was running out. The dogs, I knew, felt this too, as we walked together in silence and intuited each other's thoughts.

Finn suddenly dashing into a thicket of alpine current. Ifrit right behind. A covey of grouse exploding into flight. Finn trotting back, saying, "God that was fun!" Ifrit wagging her tongue in agreement. Nobie saying, "The noise scared me." Panda calls Nobie a sissy.

On reaching the spring, Ifrit says, "You took your suitcase out of the closet this morning. Please, His Nibs (which is what I imagine she called me), don't go."

"You might not come back!" Nobie cries.

"You might forget about us," Panda adds.

"Who'd take us on hikes then?" Finn asks.

I, sitting on my favorite log, reply, "I've got to go, Niblets, to earn money to pay for your Milk Bones. But don't worry, I'll be back soon. And I'll miss you every moment.

Nobie protesting, "We'll stop eating Milk Bones if you'll stay!"

Ifrit sitting up facing me, whispers almost to herself, "We'll miss you too, no matter how long you're gone."

Finn breaking in, "Hey gang, there's a squirrel!"

The four dashing off in hot pursuit.

Or so I imagined those interludes, as life got busier and time began to run out.

* * * * *

I had left for town on errands. Diana stood at hitching post, saddling Dandy. As Nobie and Panda milled around them a Federal Express truck arrived, delivering an unexpected package with research materials for my next column. Nobie and Panda ran at truck. The driver, who was looking towards the house and not in the direction of the hitching post, didn't see them coming. His truck hit Nobie, killing him instantly.

Just like that, he was gone. When I returned, Diana greeted me at the back porch. "Something terrible's happened," she said.

A huge hole had opened. Until that moment we hadn't realized what a big space Nobie had filled. His quirks had made him impossible to ignore during life. And their absence made him impossible to forget in death. His inconsolable vulnerabilities left us with a terrible sense of incompleteness. A unique soul we had so wanted to convince was loved, who died before he knew. The hurt wouldn't stop.

We buried Nobie by the stream behind our house in a grove of cottonwood and aspen. We lined his grave with grass, placed a slate marker over it, and returned often to visit.

* * * * *

In an effort to console ourselves after Nobie's death, we acquired another dog—the giant Schnauzer, "MacDuff." German dogs, we heard, were the least in-bred and MacDuff was German. And whether that generalization is true or not, he grew to be among the most outstanding dogs we ever had. Bright and affectionate, he attached himself to Diana. Possessing a great sense of humor, he found many ways to make us laugh. On hikes he liked to pick up big sticks—the bigger the better—and carry them home. Many were six feet long or longer. Our efforts to convince him that giant dogs must keep "four on the floor" were only half-success-ful. We compromised at two feet. Hence, we often found him sprawled across our king-size double bed, his hind feet barely touching the floor, and his front feet almost reaching the other side.

MacDuff joined our hikes and walk-rides, providing protection for the JRs, and merriment for all. But his presence erased neither our grief over Nobie nor our growing fear that Finn and Ifrit's line might die out. Ifrit, almost ten, was too old to breed again, and Panda, at four, had just a couple of breeding years left. There was little time left to ensure our own variant of Finn and Ifrit's "genetic immortality."

This didn't mean replicating them through line breeding, as some Parson Russell breeders did. Incest, we knew, didn't immortalize anything. Rather, we hoped to breed Panda to an entirely unrelated, sporting terrier. And while this wouldn't guarantee Finn and Ifrit much immortality it would ensure the pups shared their genes, and inherited the qualities of intelligence, stamina, courage, and ability we so admired.

But we couldn't find Panda a mate. The only males we saw in Montana were Parson Russell types—too long of leg and short on muscle and stamina. The transformation of Jack Russells into show dogs and pets now threatened the future of our own terriers.

Then, just three months after Nobie's death, our hopes to breed Panda were suddenly dashed. During her heat, a neighbor's poodle achieved a lock. Fearing that birthing pups of a much larger dog might be danger-ous, the vet gave Panda an abortion pill. This caused a uterine infection; and to save her life we had her spayed.

Finn, Ifrit, and Panda would be the last of the line. Our efforts to en-sure their "genetic immortality" had failed and once again we faced the prospect, as we had after Phineas' death, that the dogs we loved would die without issue.

But if biology can't guarantee dogs a life after death, what could?

Alston with Panda and Ifrit, 1987
"Ifrit, almost ten, was too old to breed again, and Panda,
at four, had just a couple of breeding years left.
There was little time left to ensure . . .
Finn and Ifrit's 'genetic immortality.'"

16

Ifrit's Spirit

*This mysterious life potency of animals which is a separate
thing from the body has always been known under various
names, yet it is commonly recognized as mind or soul, and as
that immaterial, immortal principle which goes to form all
animal life,*

> —*E. D. Buckner,*
> The Immortality of Animals, *1903*

*For love that comes wherever life and sense
Are given to God, in thee was most intense;*

> —*William Wordsworth,*
> *"To the Memory of Little Music"*

For Ifrit it was a day like many others, filled with love, play, empathy,
anxiety, courage, and near sudden death.

She greeted the dawn by thoroughly washing Panda's face. As usual,
she was methodical. She licked her daughter's left ear, then her face and
eyes, and ended with a complete scrub of the right ear. Only then did she
deem Panda sufficiently presentable to go outside and do potty.

After breakfast came the rumpus run: Starting slowly, she slalomed
around the living room furniture, then coursed down the hall into the bedroom and took a flying leap onto our bed before heading back to the living
room. By the second lap she was smoking, tongue out. And by the third
her energy had created such a strong magnetic field that it drew Panda and
MacDuff into its orbit (Finn declined to join, having decided such scampers
undignified), thus creating exactly the chaos and joy she intended.

Then Ifrit took her post at my feet in the study. And while pretending
to sleep, she was actually at work. Her job, as she saw it, was to be a

kind of psychic watchdog: to keep a close ear and eye on my mood and remain alert to any nuance of voice or body that signaled trouble. And sure enough, that day being a Monday, there was.

At eleven, the editor of my weekly newspaper column called to say she was leaving the office early and that I needed to get my copy to her for editing by three o'clock. As I hadn't started it yet, this news had the effect of concentrating my mind considerably. And of course, Ifrit sensed my panic. As I tensed and hunched over the keyboard, she tensed and hunched over the rug, hanging her head lugubriously and quaking like an aspen in the breeze. Only when the column was done and safely on its way by fax (this being before the Internet), did she revive. Sitting up at my feet she said with more eloquence than I could ever muster, "Can we play our gopher game now?"

The gopher game had been our mutual invention. One day on a hike I noticed that Ifrit, being only eleven inches high, had trouble seeing gophers in the tall grass. She needed an observation platform high enough to see over it, much like the ones the English Raj used for hunting tigers. By mutual consent, it was decided I'd be that platform. And it worked spectacularly. I held her under my arm and began walking through the field. Almost immediately, she saw a gopher by its hole, sunning itself. I pointed Ifrit at the animal, aiming her like a gun, then put her on the ground. She was on the rodent in a trice, dispatching it with a few shakes of her head.

That first morning we had bagged thirteen gophers in an hour and the "gopher game" was born. But this day the conditions weren't right. In clear weather gophers leave their holes to sun themselves. But when it's cloudy such as today they stay underground. We decided to hike with Finn, Panda, and MacDuff instead.

* * * * *

In the mountains above our place there's a diversion dam that gathers the waters of the South Fork of Deep Creek and directs them into an irrigation ditch which carries them downhill. Along the way they're diverted again and again, into progressively smaller rivulets that course through meadows, feeding the thirst of ranch grass and alfalfa. The ditch was built by a lady named Anna Ryan in 1882 and has been used ever since. And having been there so long it doesn't appear to be a ditch: Thickets of willow and large cottonwood trees crowd its banks, making it look like an entirely natural mountain stream.

In spring, when melting snow brings the South Fork to flood, the ditch is transformed into a torrent that tumbles downhill faster than a man can run and too deep to stand in. Just above our fence, a diversion box divides the ditch in two, funneling the water so that it picks up even more speed. And lying across this box is a single, foot-wide board that serves as a bridge, allowing people and dogs to cross to the other side.

That's where, that day, Ifrit had her accident.

The dogs and I had just started across when Finn, always in a hurry, brushed past us. He accidentally nudged Ifrit, who lost her balance and tumbled head first into the churning water. She bobbed to the surface briefly, looking terrified, then was swept from sight. I raced after her but heavy stands of willow lining the ditch obscured my view. For an instant I saw her, clinging desperately to a root, and then she lost her grip and was swept down-ditch once more. Further along I saw her again, traveling in the current faster than I could run.

I was losing the race, and it was a race against more than time. Not far below, the ditch went into a large irrigation pipe. If she were sucked into it she would be gone forever. Then I spotted her again. She had scrambled halfway up a steep, muddy bank but was now slipping backward into the water. I arrived just in time to sweep her into my arms.

* * * * *

This was Ifrit's irony. A small fluff of a thing, less than fourteen pounds, not terribly strong, who suffered periodic anxiety attacks and diarrhea throughout life, Ifrit nevertheless found more ways to get herself nearly killed than any dog we'd ever known. Possessing so much courage and heart, she accepted challenges she didn't have the strength to meet. And this regularly put her in danger. Besides the usual porcupine quillings and numerous near-calamities with badgers, coyotes, foxes, moose, and raccoons, she found many novel ways to tempt fate as well.

She loved mountain climbing but had bad balance.

She loved the high alpine country where the thin atmosphere exposed her to harmful solar radiation, and once fell victim to snow blindness and sunstroke.

She loved to hike with the horses but followed so close behind they often stepped on her feet.

She loved to accompany me cross-country skiing, even though being so short she often disappeared in snowdrifts.

But water was her special weakness. She loved it with a passion even though she could barely swim. Her short legs were unable to produce sufficient forward propulsion. So rather than swimming forward she merely

Ifrit at Blue Spring, June 1987
"A small fluff of a thing, less than fourteen pounds . . .
Ifrit nevertheless found more ways to get herself nearly killed
than any dog we'd ever known."

"Water was her special weakness."

treaded water until she tired and began to sink and only her black nose remained above the surface, bobbing like a waterlogged cork.

Three times Ifrit nearly drowned in the Smith, twice in the drainage ditch, countless times in the South Fork, and once in a mountain lake. Twice, while fishing with me on the Spring Creek, she got so excited about a trout I was playing that she dove into the fast water and was carried downstream toward the creek's confluence with the turbulent Yellowstone River. Each time, I reached her just as she was about to plunge into the boiling rapids.

Ifrit had so many narrow escapes that as the years wore on Diana and I actually worried less about her. We'd grown accustomed to her brushes with death and began unconsciously to assume she'd live forever. Her physical vulnerabilities shrank in significance as her spiritual qualities loomed larger until we came to see her not as a physical being at all, but a spirit. And spirits, we told ourselves, do not age or die.

* * * * *

Yet by 1990 both Finn and Ifrit began to fade. He developed a heart murmur—perhaps a consequence of the two near-fatal maulings by Annie. And while he gamely continued to hike, his gentle rocking-horse canter that had long been so effortless became slow and labored.

Ifrit's night vision and hearing declined. But being in denial about her aging we failed to notice. We didn't even see the significance of yet another near-death experience, when, in her deafness, until the last split second she failed to hear my frantic cries of warning or the thunderous steps of a dog-hating mule that had raced up behind her with savage intent.

So Ifrit's decline continued. The following summer she lost interest in hikes. She walked with me and the other dogs to the front gate, then turned and went back to the house. Throughout early fall she came down with various small ailments, necessitating frequent visits to the vet: diminished appetite and weight loss; a cyst behind an ear, lameness on one hind leg. On November 7th, I took her to Dr. Ron Stafford, our vet, to check the leg and he found something else.

17

Ifrit Passes

Do you look for me at times,
Wistful ones?
Do you look for me at times
Strained and still?
Do you look for me at times,
When the hour for walking chimes,
On that grassy path that climbs
Up the hill?

> —*Thomas Hardy,*
> *"Dead 'Wessex' the Dog to the Household"*

If we have spirits that persist—they have. If we know
after our departure who we were—they do.

> —*John Galsworthy,*
> *"Memories,"* The Inn of Tranquility, *1912*

Dr. Stafford stood on the other side of the examination table and lifted Ifrit's short, cropped tail. Her bottom was covered with tell-tail brown stains.

"She has diarrhea," he said.

"Probably just her nervous tummy," I replied.

But a week later, despite medication her diarrhea hadn't gone away. Then Stafford's partner, Dr. Greg Lovgren called with bad news. Blood tests confirmed her kidneys were failing.

We put her on a prescription diet designed for kidney disease but her system couldn't tolerate the new food and she vomited it up. We tried another medicine which for a while seemed to work. Briefly, her old cheerfulness returned. But by early December, she was shaking uncontrollably.

On Saturday, December 7th I was scheduled to fly to California for research on my next book, *In a Dark Wood*. I didn't want to leave with Ifrit so ill, but my ticket was non-refundable, and besides, I still refused to believe she was mortally ill. She had just turned thirteen, I reminded myself, and that was young for a JR.

Remaining determinedly optimistic, I decided to take the trip. On Friday I packed my suitcase in preparation for an early flight the next morning. Then Diana and I decided to go out briefly for dinner. Before leaving the house, I took Ifrit outside to relieve herself.

It was bitterly cold and dark. A ferocious wind blew. As she stood by the back steps she looked up at me, so trusting, so sad, so weak, shivering in the cold winter darkness. I wanted to cry. In retrospect, I should have realized she knew she was about to die and wanted to say goodbye. But still in denial about her condition, we went to dinner anyway. As she could hold neither her bladder nor bowels, we left her in the bathroom.

When we returned at 9:00pm we found her dead on the bathroom floor. I missed my chance to say goodbye.

* * * * *

At 5:00am the next morning, I left for the airport and California, grieving every minute. As the ground was frozen, Diana carefully wrapped her body and put it in the locker freezer to await the spring thaw. And on my return from California, I wrote a eulogy of Ifrit in my syndicated newspaper column

Her name was Ifrit. And last week she taught me a lesson about Christmas.

Ifrit was a fuzzy little white dog, a Jack Russell terrier, weighing about fourteen pounds. Her name refers to a supernatural creature described in the "Arabian Nights." According to that classic fable, ifrits are mischievous female genies who mysteriously appear, changing people into horses or frogs or trees (or vice versa), before vanishing. So too the Ifrit of my story suddenly materialized, transforming me before departing.

Jack Russell terriers are canine pocket rockets. Not much larger than a football, they pack the energy of a 250 pound linebacker. Sometimes described as "miniature rhinoceroses on amphetamines," they suffer from the illusion that they outweigh Great Danes. They demand to be treated with respect, or else the transgressor is likely to lose a finger. Anyone who has lived with a JR knows who is boss.

But Ifrit was different. She was a kinder and gentler JR. We met in January, 1979. I was in New Jersey doing research for a book. One rainy Sunday afternoon a friend and I visited a nearby kennel. There must have been forty pups in the place. But only one locked her gaze on me. This fuzzy little seven-week-old fur ball, about the size of a guinea pig, pushed past a half dozen competitors and insisted I take her home to Montana.

Once home, Ifrit never left my side. She even gave birth to a litter of pups in my lap. She was my muse, helping me write more than a million words over a decade. She would sit in my lap, pressing her head against my chest and fix her eyes on me as I plinked at the word processor.

Extremely intelligent and using eloquent body language, she had a larger vocabulary than the average college freshman. And she read me like a book. She knew when I was happy or sad. She knew, at the end of each writing day when I performed a "backup" on my computer, signaling it was time to take a hike and get on with the more important business of eating supper.

And she knew how to bring joy. Sure, she could be a terror. Like all JRs, she was a terrific hunter, petrifying the marmots and gophers who surround our house. Once while playing she bit me so hard I had to get a tetanus shot. But despite her feistiness she had a limitless capacity for love; and unlike many JRs—who take themselves too seriously—she knew how to laugh.

In our household, containing five dogs and two crusty humans, she was the catalyst who melded and transformed our individual moodiness into a cheerful communal chemistry.

Usually she spread her cheer by giving everyone a little kiss each morning. But when that was insufficient to chase our blues away, she insisted on playing games. She would do anything for a laugh: sit up, roll, or run around the house as though her stubby tail was on fire. She kept this up until everyone—dogs and people alike—had joined her.

But she was never robust. We lived with a dread certainty that one day this irreplaceable creature would die. She had many bouts with intestinal illness, nearly succumbing several times. But she always bounced back, as cheerful as ever. Until last week.

On December 6th, exactly one week past her 13th birthday, Ifrit died. Just a few days earlier her kidneys suddenly failed. My wife and I tried everything to save her. Eventually we found a treatment that seemed to help. For a while she showed her old perkiness, nodding her head at us as if to say, "Come on, cheer up." But not long after was dead.

We miss Ifrit terribly. Eventually we may find other dogs whom we will love, perhaps even as much. But none will replace Ifrit. Combining intelligence, humor, bravery, vulnerability, and an infinite capacity for love, she proved that individual animals have personalities as unique and different as humans. No matter how hard dog breeders may try to produce a certain canine disposition, they ultimately fail. The individuality of dogs, like that of people and other creatures, cannot be suppressed.

Ifrit reminded me this season that life is a miracle, a gift, which rewards us with love. The story of Christmas—about birth and rebirth and loving one another—contains a message for the entire earth. Every living thing is unique and precious and deserves our respect. We are born and eventually we die. But in between, if we are lucky, we may briefly encounter special creatures like Ifrit who teach us to love and give us joy.

* * * * *

On a hot day the following August we carried Ifrit's little body to the grove under the cottonwoods. Finn and Panda came along. Sun filtered through the tall trees, casting a phantasmagoria of light and shadow on the ground. I held her to my breast and stroked her. She felt as good to hold as when she was alive. I did not want to let go. I placed her in the grave next to Nobie's on my old, white sweater which she had slept on while lying at my feet in the study. She seemed asleep.

Finn stood by, looking at Ifrit intently. He understood. I covered her body with grass and Diana laid a cottonwood branch on top of her. After we buried her, Finn did not want to leave. I went back to the house for the wheelbarrow, which I filled with rocks to place on the grave. When I returned, Finn was still there, watching over her.

18

Daisy and Bungee

Everyone can master a grief but he that has it.
> —*William Shakespeare,*
> *"Much Ado about Nothing"*

Now I would ask her, for love of me, to have another. It would be a poor tribute to my memory never to have a dog again.
> —*Eugene O'Neill,*
> The Last Will and Testament of an Extremely
> Distinguished Dog

As the months passed following Ifrit's death, my grief did not abate. She had been *the special* dog of my life and I was convinced we'd never find another like her. Of her family, only Panda remained; and she would leave no progeny.

Nevertheless, we found ourselves praying for a miracle. Could she be reincarnated?

For more than 3,000 years, belief in the persistence of the soul after death and reincarnation has guided the thoughts of many of the world's philosophies and religions. It appeared in Hinduism's Upanishads as early as 1,000 B.C., and it was a recurring theme in ancient Greek religion and philosophy beginning with the foundation of the Orphic religion in the sixth century, B. C. Variations of it appeared in the Idealist philosophies of Pythagoras and Plato.

According to this tradition, Orpheus was a musician with supernatural powers and the only mortal the god permitted to visit the underworld where the dead reside. When Orpheus' wife, Eurydice, died, he descended to the underworld and asked Hades, the ruler of the underworld, if he could have her back. Hades agreed, giving Orpheus permission to lure

On a hot day, Daisy cools off at "Daisy's Dip."
"Daisy quickly showed herself every inch a sporting terriers."

Eurydice to the world of the living by playing his lyre. But, Hades warned, when Orpheus led Eurydice upward he must not look back or she would disappear forever. Orpheus followed Hades' instructions until he and Eurydice had almost reached the upper world. Then, overcome with curiosity, he looked back. In an instant Eurydice vanished forever.

In Orphism, the souls of all living things—animals and people—are immortal. While the body lives, the soul remains imprisoned in the body. But when the body dies, the soul is freed. Bad souls remain underground, but good souls can reenter a new body of their choosing.

The Orphic religion would influence Greek thinkers for the next several centuries, including Plato. In his philosophic classic, *The Republic*, written around 360 BC, Plato tells the story of a warrior named Er who was killed in battle. But despite being left on the battlefield for ten days, his body did not decay, and just before burial, he came back to life. The gods gave him back life, he told his astonished family, so that he might tell them what happens to the soul after death.

According to Er, after he died he found himself in a "marvelous meadow," where he met people "encamped like pilgrims at a festival." In the meadow, there were four openings, one leading downward to the underworld; the second up from it; the third upward to the sky, and the fourth descending from it. Between these openings sat judges who passed sentence on the dead, commanding some to go down into the underworld where they had to serve out terms of varying lengths as punishment. The good were allowed to take the exit that led to the sky and took them to another marvelous place. Eventually, all returned to the meadow, then went to another place where they were told, "here shall begin a new round of earthly life, to end in death. No guardian spirit will cast lots for you, but you shall choose your own destiny." Souls could decide what body they'd next like to occupy.

* * * * *

But these were just myths, we told ourselves. The temptation to believe them was a symptom of grief. Dogs cannot be reincarnated. Cloning's impossible. There's no "ghost in the machine," just a machine. What is gone is gone forever. Rather than wait for Ifrit to return we'd have to replace her.

I called Marilyn Veile. "Do you have any Jack Russells related to Ifrit?" I asked. She didn't. Her husband had just died. She'd resigned as manager of the Hamilton Farm kennel and was moving to Florida to live with her sister. But she might have a dog for me. During the move she

Daisy as Pup, Spring 1992
"She carried a certain sadness in her soul."

left her own Jack Russell, Goliath, with a friend in Aiken South Carolina, Nancy Lee Ellis, who specialized in producing sporting Jack Russells. Mrs. Ellis planned to breed Goliath to her bitch, Aiken Question. And Marilyn promised to let me have a female from that litter.

On February 14th, Aiken Question whelped, and on April 16th, Diana and I drove to Bozeman airport to pick up the pup. When her plane arrived and we opened the crate, we encountered a skinny, smooth-coated little terrier, with lovely brown markings on her face, looking very worried and lonely.

We decided to call this simple little flower, "Daisy."

Daisy quickly showed herself every inch a sporting terrier. Mrs. Ellis bred her dogs for the local foxhunting community and regularly out-crossed to ensure genetic and sporting strength. So Daisy would remain throughout her life a phenomenal athlete with stamina and hunting instinct that never quit. In one week when just five months old she scaled 10,289-foot Ramshorn Peak with me, then two days later accompanied me on a ten-mile hike to a mountain lake nearly 10,000 feet above sea level. On these treks she was impossible to control, ranging out of sight at high speed in search of game as I called in vain for her.

Aggressively affectionate, Daisy showered attention on anyone who came to the door. Yet she carried a certain sadness in her soul. As Mrs. Ellis had been old and ill when the pup was born, she was whelped at a boarding kennel. The pup never had the love every young dog needs from birth. So she grew to have a craving for love that couldn't be quenched.

And I made matters worse. For while Daisy was nearly the perfect dog—affectionate, athletic, and never sick a day in her life—for me she had a terrible flaw: she wasn't Ifrit. In fact, she was almost exactly the opposite of Ifrit: smooth rather than rough coated, tough rather than gentle, and independent rather than a constant companion. Yet Daisy was all I had. So, while I still grieved over Ifrit, I tried hard to love Daisy as much and hide my disappointment. I took her everywhere. She spent days on the couch beside my desk and evenings on our bed under the pillow that lay between Diana and me.

* * * * *

Then one day when Daisy was two she attacked Panda. As Reverend Russell, Alys Serrell, and Jocelyn Lucas knew, sporting Jack Russells can be very aggressive. Fighting is normal. That's one reason why the Jack Russell Terrier Club of America strongly urges that no family with children under six keep a JR, as the sudden movements of, or tormenting by, children can sometimes trigger an attack.

And JRs far more frequently direct this aggression towards their own kind. Females especially are inclined to fight each other, being driven by the "alpha female" reproductive instinct. JR bitches are especially prone to fight when let through a door together. The opening of any door excites a JR, who is driven by competitive instinct to get through first. And in these circumstances, younger females are likely to attack older ones.

But we knew none of this then. Occasionally Panda had launched a mock attack on Ifrit, but her forays were so gentle we paid no attention. But Daisy wasn't gentle. Until she was two, she and Panda had got along fine. They hiked and slept on our bed together. Then one day, as we left on a hike and the dogs were in high state of anticipatory excitement, I let them through the door together. Daisy grabbed the four-inch shorter Panda by the back of the neck and held on with a vice-like grip. It took considerable twisting of her collar and the use of leather gloves to separate them. Panda was left with a deep puncture wound.

Despite our efforts to prevent further attacks, they occasionally reoccurred. Panda grew afraid of Daisy. We later understood that we shouldn't have blamed Daisy for this behavior. She was behaving as sporting terriers do. But when she began hurting gentle Panda, it was hard to love her as much. And Daisy sensed our disappointment. She looked at me as if to say, "What have I done wrong? Please tell me and I'll change." She tried so hard to please.

* * * * *

So as Daisy failed to fill the void in my heart, despite myself I prayed for Ifrit's reincarnation. Then two weeks later I received a call from a young college student from Texas named Mark Kollock. "I read the column you wrote about Ifrit in the Dallas newspaper," he told me, "and I know a dog just like her—short, gentle, rough-coated. The dog's name is Cricket. I have one of her pups. She belongs to a couple in Denton named John and Terri Zagrodnick. And she's just whelped a second time. Perhaps one from that litter might be just like Ifrit."

Was a miracle in the offing? Already, Kollock's call culminated what seemed an improbable chain of events: that he read my December column, recognized Ifrit's and Cricket's similarities, searched and found my phone number and called me four months after the column appeared.

I phoned the Zagrodnicks. "Cricket's litter is spoken for," Terri told me. "But we'll probably breed again in the fall. Stay in touch."

Bungee at Five Weeks, January 1993
"We chose a male from Cricket's litter
and decided to call him, 'Bungee.'"

Terri called in December to say the third litter arrived on the eighth. Two males and a female. She sent pictures.

"I'm looking for a pup just like my Ifrit," I told her. "What are the chances one from this litter might resemble her?"

"Anything's possible," she replied. And she knew. For she was convinced Cricket herself was the reincarnation of a dog she once dearly loved who disappeared.

"I firmly believe in reincarnation," she told me later. "I believe that Cricket is a reincarnation of a little mixed breed dog I had back in the early '70s that was lost in the shuffle of a divorce. Neither my ex-husband nor I could keep her and we gave her to his parents. They left her in the back yard overnight while they left town. When they returned she was gone with no obvious holes dug under the fence. So she was lost forever. Her name was Wendy . . . It was a most painful experience . . . When Cricket came [in 1990] there were so many times that she reminded me of Wendy, and one day I asked her outright, 'Are you my Wendy?' and her eyes squinted just a bit as she smiled at me."

We chose a male from Cricket's litter and decided to call him, "Bungee." He arrived at the Bozeman airport on February 2nd, 1993 in a crate that Terri had decorated with colored ribbons and an inscription over its door that said, "Bungee of Millegan's home."

Bungee did not exactly resemble Ifrit. Although like her short-legged and rough-coated, he was more beautiful. In fact, he was the cutest, fuzziest little pup we'd ever seen, with a handsome brown and black muzzle and dark mascara-like lining around the eyes. But otherwise he seemed her clone.

Born a year and two days after she died, it was difficult not to imagine her soul had returned in his body. He jumped into my arms as though he'd known me for years. For the rest of his life he would never voluntarily leave me, as though our every waking movement together was precious to him. Like Ifrit, he slept on top of my foot when I worked at my desk. Even as a tiny pup, he taught himself to sit up on his haunches as Ifrit did. Like her, he exuded joy, trotting ahead of me on hikes with a happy one-two-three-skip hippity-hop trot. And he played like her—bringing me rocks to throw for him to retrieve. And, like her, he became my fishing buddy.

My prayers had been answered. But was Bungee really Ifrit reincarnate? I neither knew nor cared. All that mattered was that he made me indescribably happy.

19

Ranching the View

No matter how deep my sleep I shall hear you,
and not all the power of death can keep my spirit
from wagging a
grateful tail.

> —*Eugene O'Neill,*
> The Last Will and Testament of an
> Extremely Distinguished Dog

But he'd stick to me till his latest breath;
An' he'd go with me to the gates of death.
He'd wait for a thousand years maybe;
Scratching the door and whining for me
If myself were inside in Purgatory.

> —*Winifred M. Letts,*
> *"Tim an Irish Terrier"*

After Ifrit died, Finn continued to mourn. He kept vigil at her grave, where we would find him staring at it with a sad expression on his scarred, graying face. His heart began to fail and he hiked less. A year after she died, we hiked together along with Panda and Daisy to Nobie's Rock. It would be his last trek. By the following spring his heart had worsened, his breathing labored, and the pain increased. At the end of April we put him to sleep and buried him under the cottonwoods next to Ifrit and Nobie. MacDuff and Panda were there. Both were very upset. Panda kept staring at the grave and refused to leave it.

I resumed my hikes with Daisy, Bungee, MacDuff, and faithful little Panda, whose short legs and stout heart would not quit. When I fished the local spring creek, Bungee came as Ifrit's replacement. Like her, he stood chest-deep in water as she had, getting as close to me as he dared as I waded out into the stream. He scanned the water's surface to search for rising trout, signaling me when he saw one by barking impatiently. And when I hooked a fish, he, unable to contain his excitement, would swim out to me and make desperate efforts to help me put the fish in the landing net.

But speaking and research trips increasingly took me away from home and our hikes and angling became less frequent. In the spring of 1994 I was gone for four months as a visiting fellow at Harvard University, and in 1997 gone again for four months to University of Maryland's School of Public Affairs. After my mother, who lived in South Carolina, died in 1995 having designated me as Personal Representative of her estate, I took countless trips south to deal with probate. Meanwhile, even while home the pressure to meet writing deadlines allowed less time for the dogs. During my absences Bungee was inconsolable. When I was home he slept as usual at my feet but increasingly sought my attention. He repeatedly sat up to catch my eye and when this failed, bounded desperately into my lap without invitation, catching me by surprise, and smothering me with kisses. Each time, I patted him, put him back on the floor, and promised to spend more time with him later. "When I finish the book," I told him, "we'll have lots of time together."

* * * * *

Meanwhile, Paradise Valley was changing. As in Millegan, the old ranch culture was dying, but whereas poverty killed Millegan, wealth doomed the valley.

The agent of change was the valley's fabulous trout fishing. In 1938 a man named Dan Bailey gave up a promising career in atomic physics to move with his wife, Helen, from New York City to Livingston, where he opened a tackle store devoted to fly fishing. In summers, many of his friends came to visit. Several were writers who published books and magazine articles celebrating the region's fabulous angling.

By the early 1960s they had put the valley on the map. It became a prime trout-fishing destination. In the late 1960s more writers moved to Livingston. Some wrote for movies and attracted Hollywood friends to the valley as well. These affluent immigrants drove up real estate values, tempting ranchers to sell. Some new arrivals formed environmental advocacy groups and began attacking ranchers as enemies of the land whose overgrazing hurt wildlife and whose irrigation drained trout streams. It was not long before these fourth generation Montanans felt under siege and began to move elsewhere.

In 1992, Robert Redford's movie, *A River Runs Through It* appeared, followed in 1998 by his *The Horse Whisperer*. Both, having been filmed in the region, accelerated the upscale immigration. Soon the bi-coastal, restless rich had followed the movie stars, buying huge spreads to "ranch the view," and building multi-million dollar second or third homes as monuments to themselves. More ranchers left and more twenty-some-things arrived to take jobs as fishing guides and restaurant waiters to serve these wealthy clients. Real estate developers appeared from other parts of the country to build subdivisions, gated communities, and golf courses.

By the late 1990s the old culture was almost gone. The rich new arrivals spent at most a few weeks a year in the valley, then locked the gates and left. Unlike the ranchers, they didn't know that the old "Code of the West" calling for neighborly cooperation was the secret of family survival and the glue that held a community together. And not living there year-round and, therefore, neither knowing nor caring that feuds over fences could poison feelings for generations; these transient ex-urbanites weren't very friendly to either people or the land.

Accustomed to gated communities and securely locked apartments, they couldn't tolerate others hiking or fishing their spreads. Not understanding the ecological importance of burning and grazing for stimulating growth of grasses and other palatable plants needed by wildlife, and disliking the smell of manure, they neither burned nor kept cattle. And not wanting to bother, they didn't irrigate.

Left unburned, ungrazed, and unirrigated, grasses died, soil dried, and weeds spread. As grasses died, pastures turned to pine forests crowding out the berries, willow, and aspen on which the diversity of wildlife depends. Only deer and elk remained abundant, and that was an embarrassment of riches. Left unchecked, their exploding populations consumed habitat that other creatures, from beaver to bear, needed. It was private enterprise's recapitulation of the Yellowstone disaster. But this time it was the rich, not bureaucrats, who did the damage.

* * * * *

These changes in turn affected our treks into the Wilderness, robbing us of solitude. No longer did the land sustain the illusion of permanency, of a universe *sub specie aeternitatus*. There was no escape from change. Now we shared the trails with vacationing hikers and mountain bikers—Generation Xers and bi-coastal yuppies arriving in their SUVs to taste Montana for a season and move on.

The valley's transformation mirrored the wider one that had left sporting Jack Russells with no job to do. No longer expected to hunt, they had been discovered by those who preferred them as fashion statements.

In 1992, the television sitcom, "Frasier" debuted, starring a Jack Russell named "Eddie," and in 1995 the PBS children's program, "Wishbone" appeared, featuring a JR that travels through history wearing period costumes. These programs showed Jack Russells as terribly appealing, but by depicting them living in apartments and wearing skirts, they also grossly distorted the dogs' true character.

The public, believing Jack Russells cuddly couch potatoes and good with children, flocked to them, often with tragic consequences for both dogs and owners. Children were sometimes bitten, the family cat killed, or other pets mauled. Soon JR rescue clubs, dedicated to finding second homes for rejected dogs, had more than they could handle.

* * * * *

The public, in short, had fallen madly in love Jack Russells, but wanted them as gentle pets, not feisty sporting dogs. And this interest vastly accelerated the terrier's transformation into a modern show breed. In 1990, the Parson Jack Russell was recognized by Great Britain's Kennel Club, and in 1997 its American counterpart was accepted by the AKC, a dog which in 2003 would be officially renamed Parson Russell terrier as well—a move done, according to its web site, "to separate the AKC Parson from the 'Jack,' a short-legged terrier."

And as the new millennium dawned, the "Parson Russell" was changing in unexpected ways. It had been less than twenty-five years since its studbook was closed and the terrier had begun to be bred to the new standards demanding taller, less "quarrelsome," and more "cautious" and "submissive" dogs. Yet not only had these intended new traits begun to appear, but other surprising and unintended features began showing up as well.

Being less aggressive than its sporting counterpart, the Parson Russell made a better pet. But it was more spindly, too. Certainly, it appeared weaker than Davies' description of Reverend Russell's Trump, whose "loins and conformation of the whole frame [were] indicative of hardihood and endurance." Moreover, the Parson Russell's coat was different. Whereas most of Reverend Russell's dogs wore rough coats, the majority of Parson Russells had smooth ones. Broken coats became the exception and truly rough coats increasingly rare.

The Parson Russell's physique and coat were apparently unintended consequences of selective breeding. Breeders had selected for height and submissiveness and produced less muscle and shorter hair. This should not have been surprising.

In genetic transmission, traits go in clusters. When breeders select for one, they often inadvertently produce another. As an example, in a forty-year experiment beginning in 1959, the Russian scientist Dmitri Belyaev sought to produce tamer silver foxes by selecting only the gentlest from each generation for breeding. And after 40 years and 45,000 foxes, he succeeded.

The resulting foxes were, according to the *American Scientist*, "docile, eager to please and unmistakably domesticated." But even though Belyaev had only selected for tameness, the breeding had changed the foxes in many other ways as well. They now resembled dogs, not foxes. They carried their tails differently, had black and white coats and floppy ears. Whereas wild foxes bred only once a year in the spring, some of Belyev's vixens mated twice a year, like dogs.

Charles Darwin called this the "law of correlation." Belyaev had selected for gentleness and quite by accident produced other traits clustered with it. As Raymond Coppinger observes, "If man goes on selecting, and thus augmenting, any peculiarity, he will almost certainly modify unintentionally other parts of the structure, owing to the mysterious laws of correlation."

* * * * *

Weakness and short hair were apparently unintended consequences of the closed studbook. What other surprises lay in store for the dog? As the ranks of sporting JRs dwindled, the urgency to reproduce our own grew. In January 1995 we bred Bungee to Daisy and held our breath. And exactly sixty-two days later Daisy's temperature dropped, indicating birth was near. I put her in my study, unfurled my sleeping bag beside her, and went to sleep.

20

The Stealth and "A" Teams

I would recommend those persons who are inclined to stagnate,
whose blood is beginning to thicken sluggishly in their veins,
to try keeping four dogs, two of which are puppies. Not leaving
them to servants; really keeping them.

—Elizabeth von Arnim,
All the Dogs of My Life, *1936*

A squeaking sound. Then again. I open my eyes and look at my watch.
2:00am. Where's Daisy? Craning my neck I see her sitting on the leather
chair above my head, licking a newborn pup. I run to the bedroom and
wake Diana, "The pups are here," I tell her. We return to my study. The
second pup emerges. Diana and I help Daisy remove the sac and clean
the pup. Then we wait—and wait. The third pup arrives at 3:30 and the
fourth at 5. Four lovely little critters.

From the first day one pup in particular stood out. A female. She had
the most beautiful head, eyes, and ears of any terrier we'd ever seen—with
a brown face and ears and a big brown spot on her back. She was preco-
cious—the first to find the teats, the first to escape the whelping pen.
From the moment her eyes opened, they followed us around the room.
Indeed, for her, eye contact was everything. Not interested in playing
with her siblings, she only wanted our attention.

One night she escaped the whelping pen—two weeks before the others
learned how—and greeted us enthusiastically as we opened the door in
the morning. She was taller than the others, but that was fine with us. Like
Russell, Serrell, and Lucas, we liked all sizes and the genetic diversity
this variety represents. We kept the pup and named her Mariposa, or
"Posy" for short. And we resolved to breed her one day. She would be
the foundation of the next generation.

Hobson at Six Weeks, May 1996

"He sat apart from the others and didn't play with them. Gentle and shy—an observer, not a doer—he reminded us of Ifrit."

We found good homes for the other three. A year later, Daisy whelped again, producing another four pups. As before, we were drawn to one in particular. A rough-coated male shorter than Posy, with a face that was half white and half dark brown and black. He sat apart from the others and didn't play with them. Gentle and shy—an observer, not a doer—he reminded us of Ifrit. We kept him, calling him "Hobson," and found homes for the others.

In July 1998, Panda's sister, Dasher, who'd gone to live with Diana's college roommate in Santa Fe, died at age fourteen. Two months later, MacDuff, Diana's soul mate, succumbed to cancer and we buried him under the cottonwoods beside Finn, Ifrit, and Nobie. Hoping to find another just like him, she bought a second Giant Schnauzer from the same breeder, naming him "MacGregor." But MacGregor was too aggressive towards the JRs, and we had to give him to friends. Trying a second time to replicate MacDuff, Diana acquired a third Giant Schnauzer, calling her "Bozzy." But Bozzy was even more dangerously aggressive than MacGregor and soon developed bladder cancer as well. After she twice attacked and nearly killed poor little Panda, we put her to sleep.

As it turned out, MacDuff's spirit had already returned—but not in the body of a Schnauzer. We had mistakenly assumed his replacement would look like him. But it was his spirit Diana had loved, and similar spirits, we discovered, can come in very different shapes and sizes.

Just six weeks after MacDuff died Daisy's third litter arrived. Five pups. After sending one—a beautifully marked, broken-coated female—to Terri Zagrodnick to live with Cricket and finding good homes for three, we kept the shortest, calling him "Chocolate." Short, rough-coated with dark brown markings and barely eleven inches tall he didn't look at all like MacDuff. But he attached himself to Diana, easing the pain of MacDuff's departure and the disappointments with MacGregor and Bozzy. And as Chocolate matured, his bond with Diana grew until she began to think MacDuff had returned after all. She stopped looking for another Schnauzer.

* * * * *

The three pups were phenomenal athletes and hunters. Otherwise, thanks to the genetic diversity of their parents and ancestors, they couldn't have been more different. Daisy was of medium height with a smooth coat and a varied sporting-dog pedigree that included, every few generations, some judicious out-crosses. Cricket was small and rough-coated; Bungee's father, Lunstar Cee Cee, taller, with a broken coat. And the

"Chocolate Ice," 2003
"Similar spirits, we discovered, can come in very
different shapes and sizes."

"Posy was all extrovert. She loved everyone and talked incessantly."

pups combined different mixtures of these attributes. No two had the same coat, height, color, conformation, or temperament.

Posy was all extrovert. She loved everyone and talked incessantly. She squealed, grunted, snored, whimpered, yipped, barked, and sometimes made a noise that sounded like gargling. She exploded with energy and dominated all the other JRs but Bungee. Yet she was extremely loving toward her younger brothers. As they grew up she helped raise them. She taught them games and let them chase her around the yard. She was kooky and eccentric as Nobie, but not as anxious. Rather than fearing thunder, she got angry at it—barking at the sky as if to shake her paw at God.

Posy invented games, nearly all of which threatened our domestic tranquility, the most cacophonous of which was "the door game."

Like her mother, Posy insisted on being the first dog through a door. But when one day I opened the south door to put her and Hobson out, she rushed through ahead of her brother, turned, and wouldn't let him pass. Of course, she had no intention of hurting Hobson, as at heart she was a gentle dog. But Hobson didn't know that. And her growling and baring of teeth, though done in fun, were enough to keep him at bay.

So when Hobson refused to breach Posy's blockade I led him through the house to the north door, to let him out there. But Posy, who remained outside, anticipated our move, and raced around the house and blocked that door too. This necessitated a mad dash back to the south door, which Hobson got through just before Posy arrived.

Thereafter, Posy played the door game at every opportunity. Carrying competitive spirit to major league levels, she blocked the door whenever another dog tried to go through. And although she did this playfully, none of the dogs—apart from Bungee, who was never deterred—dared try. When they saw her waiting to pounce, they held back. So letting the dogs out became a race from door to door and back again—and again—as Posy, anticipating our moves, raced to get there first.

The game got increasingly complicated: We tried faking a run for the second door, and when Posy rushed off to get there ahead of us we doubled back to the first. Soon, however, she caught on and wouldn't fall for the fake. So we resorted to double fakes: make a feint to the second door, double back to the first, then quickly turn around again and head for the second.

While Posy was unstoppable, Hobson proved sensitivity incarnate. Often, when we left the house even if just for a few hours, he'd have an anxiety attack that sent him deep under the covers of our bed. He yearned to be close to me, but Bungee wouldn't let him. As he feared to hike with his father, I divided the JRs into two hiking teams: the "A Team" consisting of Daisy, Bungee, and Posy; and the "Stealth Team," comprising Hobson, Chocolate, and Panda.

The loud and the quiet, the indomitable and the gentle.

21

Bungee's Summer

My dog comes racing to me, ears alert,
Jaws open in a moment of pure joy,
Long legs comb August broom and skirt
The fringe of grasses spread as its alloy,
At one with life, exuberant he lives
A purity of joy I cannot share.

—Olwen Way,
"A Shakespearian Sonnet for Ted"

Ten years ago she split the air
To seize what she could spy;
Tonight she bumps against a chair,
Betrayed by milky eye.
She seems to pant, Time up, time up!
My little dog must die,
And lie in dust with Hector's pup;
So, presently, must I.

—Ogden Nash

The sun was just peeking above Emigrant Peak when Michael Simon, Bungee, and I arrived at Len's Lake. Rays of soft morning light filtered through the cottonwoods as I unpacked my fly rod and Michael, his camera gear. Bungee stood by, watching us intently.

Len's was a private lake set at the foot of this mountain at the edge of Paradise Valley. It offered excellent fly fishing for a fee. But we weren't paying guests. Michael, a professional artist and photographer, had been hired by the lake's owners to take pictures of a fisherman catching big trout that could be used for advertising. I was to be that fisherman. My assignment was to land big rainbow trout while Michael snapped the action with his Nikon.

Bungee and I waded into the lake as Michael sat on the shore viewing us through a telephoto lens. As the water was very shallow—less than a foot even fifty feet from shore—Bungee stayed with me, alertly watching the surface for rising trout. And he was the first to see them. By the bank to our left in the shade of a large cottonwood, tiny dimples disturbed the surface. Bungee began to shiver with excitement. Being an experienced fisherman, he knew that since the smaller the rise the bigger the fish, these trout must be huge. Letting out line, I cast a small fly that landed next to the dimples. The next instant the water dimpled again and the fly disappeared.

I raised my rod and the water exploded. A large rainbow trout shot six feet into the air. Bungee, beside himself with excitement and convinced I could not possibly land such a large fish without his help, wallowed through the water towards the fish. Meanwhile, Michael remained on shore, snapping pictures.

"Bungee, stay," I ordered, and he, having had just enough obedience training to know what the command meant but not enough to take it seriously, hesitated only briefly, then continued to lunge forward. Fortunately, at that moment the trout decided to visit the other side of the lake, taking my fly and line with him. My reel screamed in protest. The trout jumped again, and again. Bungee jumped again and again too, in excitement. Eventually, the trout tired. As I led it to my waiting net, Bungee, having no confidence I could beach the fish unaided, insisted on helping. He slashed through the water and snapped at the fish, which fortunately had sufficient remaining energy to escape his attack.

"Bungee," I said sternly, "cool it." This was not a command in his vocabulary at all, but he understood the tone of my voice and hesitated. I scooped the rainbow into the net and took it ashore for Michael to capture on film. Twenty inches! Then gently lifting the trout I released it unharmed into the water. At this, Bungee, who never liked the idea of "catch and release" and thinking I'd gone completely mad, made one last effort to snare the fish in his mouth. And when the trout slipped past him the dog shot a withering backward glance at me, as if to say, "Now see what you've done!"

* * * * *

As the day wore on Bungee and I continued to stalk and catch trout and argue about how best to land a fish while Michael trailed behind with

Alston and Bungee Landing Trout, Len's Lake, July 1999
"As the day wore on, Bungee and I continued to stalk
and catch trout and argue about the best way to land a fish."

his camera. When the sun grew high and hot we stopped under a lone pine, where Michael and I shared our sandwiches with our four-legged friend. And when the sun finally dipped beneath the blue-green Gallatin Mountains and the sky turned pink and long shadows faded into the blue light of evening, we knew it had been a day to remember.

Occasionally, misfortune brings good luck. And 1999 was such a time. That spring, I suddenly found myself broke and out of work. My publisher and I, having reached an impasse on how I should write my next book, mutually agreed to void our contract. I was free as a bird, with no obligation other than to repay the publisher's advance. Having no book to write, I decided to take six months off, living on early withdrawals from my IRA. For the first time in years I had plenty of time to hike, fish, and enjoy the company of my canine friends. That day at Len's Lake was one of these dividends.

On our way home, Bungee, always nervous about my driving, shivered in my lap and refused to look at the road ahead. Nevertheless, the future looked bright. Not yet seven, Bungee was in the prime of life. We could look forward to many more days like this.

And indeed, that magic year continued. For the remainder of the summer and into the early fall we explored new trails and climbed to high mountain lakes, as I watched Bungee dance ahead on the trail, with his joyful hippity-hop skip-step. In August, we trekked alone to Davis Creek Divide, where we lunched under limber pine and basked in the warm, silent, invisible glow of intimacy that comes at these special times. We stalked wary brown trout in spring creeks and hooked and lost countless monster rainbows in remote ranch ponds. We continued to bicker about the wisdom of catch and release. We followed mountain streams to their source high above the tree line, where we dropped flies at fat cutthroat trout that lay waiting for us in the foam behind the rocks. And as the days grew shorter, our attachment reached new levels.

From the beginning, Bungee, like Ifrit, had what Diana and I called, the "loyalty gene." He never willingly left my side. He sat at my feet in the study and on my feet in bed. He accompanied me on trips to the bathroom. A day didn't pass that he wouldn't insist on playing catch with a tennis ball or rock. And when he decided I'd ignored him too long he'd sit up and fix me with a gaze of passionate intensity—seemingly knowing this had been Ifrit's old trick and thus, by reminding me of her, would render me helpless to resist his attentions.

Throughout 1999 his attachment to me continued to grow until by fall it seemed almost desperate—as though he feared that if I left the room he might never see me again. In earlier years, I'd have supposed my long absences had triggered this anxiety. But now, after our having been together daily for nearly a year I began to wonder: Was it something else?

* * * * *

"Is there something wrong with Bungee?" Bob Greenwood asked. "He looks like he's running out of gas."

We were climbing to Pine Creek Lake that sunny September 2000 day, always a long slog. At 10,000 feet in elevation, the lake was even higher than Davis Creek Divide and the trail steeper. And whether Bungee was out of breath or not, Bob and I were. Every ten steps we stopped to gasp for air. But I hadn't noticed Bungee flagging. He seemed to be trudging along just in front of me as he always did.

Yet Bob's question cut like a knife. For I had reason to worry: Did he see something I had missed?

For the past six months, Bungee had kept me on an emotional roller coaster. In March he began to lose weight. Blood tests revealed mild hepatitis. But at first it didn't seem a cause for alarm. Other than the small weight loss, he didn't seem sick. He showed none of the usual outward signs of hepatitis, such as vomiting, diarrhea, fatigue, or jaundice. Probably a temporary autoimmune problem, Dr. Stafford thought. He prescribed the anti-inflammatory, prednisone.

By June, Bungee's liver tests showed great improvement and by August, still more; but Bungee's hair was falling out. "A side-effect of the Prednisone," Stafford said, "Nothing to worry about." Nevertheless, he advised, while Bungee was on the drug, "You'd better not breed him. Prednisone affects sperm count."

* * * * *

So when Bob, Bungee, and I climbed to Pine Creek Lake that day, there was plenty to worry about. Bob, who had never been told about Bungee's illness, noticed, or thought he noticed, Bungee's fatigue—a classic symptom of liver disease. And now we'd learned his ability to procreate was at risk as well.

When Panda had been spayed, thus ending Finn and Ifrit's line, we realized our search for their "genetic immortality" had been a foolish hope. There are too many ways dogs can die without warning or lose their ability to reproduce. Yet, as Bungee and Daisy had given us three wonderful litters we couldn't help hoping to keep their line going. So after neutering Hobson and Chocolate we had begun to look for a mate for Posy.

"From the beginning, Bungee, like Ifrit, had what Diana and I called,
'the loyalty gene.' He never willingly left my side."

Bungee Watching Trout Rise, Pine Creek Lake, September 14, 2000
"When Bob, Bungee, and I climbed to Pine Creek Lake that day,
there was plenty to worry about."

But we couldn't find one. The transformation of the Jack Russells into line-bred dogs that was rocking the terrier world had once again intruded into our own lives. For while JRs had become exceedingly popular and abundant, all we could find as possible mates for Posy were "Parson Russell" types—smooth-coated, spindly wusses without muscle or stamina. Try as we might, we couldn't find a sporting JR for her. Those who kept sporting terriers did not advertise in magazines or on the Internet. They were, for the most part, private families living in foxhunting communities. But no such fraternities existed in Montana.

We kept promising Posy we'd find her a husband. With such a loving and generous temperament, she would have been a terrific mother. But as we hunted unsuccessfully for a mate, her biological clock continued to tick. When she turned six the following spring it would run out. At that age she'd be too old to breed for the first time. So rather than breed Posy we had hoped to put Bungee and Daisy together again, to produce another sire who could pass on their genes.

But now Bungee's illness was putting this plan in jeopardy. Once again, it seemed our quest for our dogs' "genetic immortality" might fail. The possibility loomed we would not only lose Bungee but his family's future as well.

* * * * *

On Stafford's advice, that fall we took Bungee off the prednisone. There was a good chance, he thought, that it had already cured Bungee and the only way to be sure was to take him off it. And indeed, a blood test in December seemed to confirm he was on the mend.

Assuming so, when Posy turned six in March we had her spayed, leaving only Daisy and Bungee to carry on their line. Then, a month later, the roller coaster plummeted again, and gathered speed. Bungee's hepatitis had returned with a vengeance. Dr. Stafford prescribed another medication, but the prognosis remained doubtful.

"If you want to breed Bungee and Daisy," Stafford said, "do it now."

* * * * *

Friday, May 18, 2001. Diana's in California attending her mother's funeral and I'm alone in house. Daisy's temperature drops and once again, I unfurl my sleeping bag on my study floor. Daisy sits on the leather chair above my head. She tosses and turns all night, but no contractions. Panting. Can't get comfortable. I'm worried. Saturday morning I call several vets but none can come.

"It's just you and me, kid," I tell her.

At noon, the first pup arrives. It's very large and gets stuck halfway. Remembering what happened to Ifrit's first, I gently pull it out and rip open the sac. A beautifully marked male, lots of color. But stillborn. An hour later, a second pup, also dead. Very small, Looks premature. After fifteen minutes a third arrives. A completely white male—and alive! But small and weak, also looking premature. At 2:45 the fourth pup emerges. A big and healthy male with dark brown on left side of face and right ear. Big brown spot on back. But blood gushes out his umbilical cord. He cries in pain.

I call the vet, who tells me I must stop the bleeding immediately or the pup will die. I try to cauterize the wound with stiptick but can't stem the flow. Holding the screaming pup in one hand, with the other I cut a length of dental floss and tie it around the hemorrhaging cord, then pull the knot tight with my teeth. The bleeding stops. As it does, Daisy delivers a fifth pup without my help. A tiny, frail female. Mostly white with one black ear and a black tail. She's too weak to suckle her mother's teat. I put evaporated milk on my little finger and hold it to her mouth. She licks.

What happened? Had Bungee's ill health affected the fetal development? Could the parents' several ties, over a period of a week or more have led to multiple conceptions, so that when the birthing occurred only two pups had reached full term? Or was the problem Daisy's age? Could one birth canal have received an inadequate blood supply, starving the fetuses in it?

I begin feeding the two smaller pups with a medicine dropper but, by Sunday, they're weaker. Not strong enough to nurse. Daisy rejects them, carrying them out of the whelping box. Diana returns home and together we feed them every three hours by dropper throughout the night. The small male dies Monday but we continue feeding the female. She, too, however, weakens and we decide to let her die. By Wednesday she's gone.

The bleeding pup survived. We thanked God for this furry little bundle and decided to call him Tigger. Without competition for his mother's milk, he grew strong and large. Long-legged like Daisy and a rough coat like Bungee, he was not only beautiful but a phenomenal athlete. At six months he was jumping over the forty-two inch high Dutch door separating the kitchen from the dining room.

Yet he was quiet and gentle—with neither Posy's madcap frenzy nor Hobson's and Chocolate's aloofness. There was sadness, too, in Tig-

Tigger at the Hidden Spring, September 1, 2002
"In our eyes he remained a miracle, a gift."

Chocolate and Hobson, January 2002
"They were loners by choice."

ger. Like Nobie, he had no littermates and missed the reassurance and security their company could give. Missing their competition at the teat, he never quite learned how to react to other dogs. Both Daisy and Posy doted on Tigger and tried to fill the void created by the loss of his brothers and sisters. But even their attention wasn't enough. While Hobson and Chocolate were loners by choice, Tigger grew that way by necessity. Suffering from an inner insecurity, he craved love but remained on guard when offered it.

But in our eyes he remained a miracle, a gift. We had our Ismail—what we hoped would be the progenitor of our next generation of JRs.

But Providence was not done. The roller coaster continued, as one surprise quickly followed another.

A month after Tigger's birth, Bungee's blood tests showed a complete recovery. Apparently, the new medicine cured him. After months of worry, we suddenly seemed to face a happy future.

A chaotic future as well. In the world of Jack Russells, six makes a critical mass and explosions would be frequent. Chocolate took an immediate dislike to Tigger and attacked him whenever possible. Unfortunately, Tigger was bigger and stronger and, although pacifist by nature, when drawn into the fray inflicted serious damage to the older, smaller dog. So we had to keep them separated, which was sometimes difficult, given the fact that Tigger could jump over the kitchen's Dutch door at a single bound. We had to keep Daisy away from Panda as well. To maintain the peace we resorted to extreme social engineering. We kept the A and Stealth Teams apart by cycling them in shifts, not only on hikes but in the kitchen and living room as well. We put a latch on Diana's study door and a baby gate on mine.

Sort of like the Berlin Wall.

22

Bungee's Winter

Remembering the joy you gave,
Dear Comrade, heavy-souled
I stand alone beside your grave,
And feel the sunshine cold

—*Cecil Floersheim,*
"*In Memory of my Dog*"

And the tear that we shed, though in secret it rolls,
Shall long keep his memory green in our souls.

—*Thomas Moore,*
Irish Melodies

By the fall of 2001 Panda's end seemed near. Now seventeen, she had been losing her sight and hearing since passing her fifteenth birthday. But her spirit never flagged and she continued to hike with the Stealth Team. Unable to see, she would veer off the trail, get lost, tumble down embankments, and fall headfirst into the creek, until the summer of 2000 when I began taking her on hikes with a leash.

But her life had become increasingly difficult. We had to accompany her whenever she went outdoors, as she got lost quickly when alone. And since she no longer had the ability to bark, she couldn't tell us where she was. Sometimes we hunted for her for hours. On one occasion, we found her stuck in a badger hole. Two other times we discovered her on the neighbor's property, walking in circles. But her stout heart remained healthy and we could not bear to put her to sleep.

So Ifrit's and Finn's last little girl soldiered on, imprisoned in her blindness and deafness, keeping us company. But we knew she had little time left.

As it turned out, we were half-right. Another dog would soon die, but not Panda. The roller coaster was about to begin its terminal descent.

* * * * *

Throughout the fall of 2001, I continued my hikes with Bungee. He seemed as energetic as ever as I watched him happily skip-step in front of me up the trail. Convinced he had survived the hepatitis, only in quiet moments did I notice a certain desperation in his gaze that seemed to say, "We haven't much time."

On Wednesday, December 26th, I recorded in my diary that in putting the dogs out before dinner, "Bungee not his usual, hyper self."

"Letting dogs out around noon," I recorded the next day:

noticed Bungee struggling in snow, seeming weak. Definitely slow. Picked him up and carried him inside. He lay gasping on sofa for several minutes, then popped up as though nothing had happened. Didn't seem sick—cold nose, still ate the end of my Fig Newton. Don't know what's the matter. Could it be the tiny scraps of ham I mixed with his breakfast the last two days? Seems unlikely. Took temperature—normal (102 degrees). At 4:00pm he hiked with me and the rest of the A Team to Nobie's Rock. Seemed usual, energetic self, running ahead skipping his left foot every three steps and hopping along doing his joyful little dance.

Bungee couldn't be seriously ill, I thought. It must just be indigestion. He was only nine—very young for a JR—and so full of life. According to his most recent blood test, we'd cured his hepatitis. And after he bounced back quickly from the fainting spell, I felt reassured, and did nothing about it.

When putting the dogs out after breakfast the following Sunday, however, Bungee acted logy and didn't want to go. As I gave him a gentle shove with my foot to urge him along, he growled softly and complainingly at me. And when a few minutes later Diana looked out the kitchen window, she saw Bungee lying in the snow. She rushed outside, shouting, "Something's' wrong with Bungee!"

I ran out and brought him into the house and put him on the sofa. He lay there panting and inert, his gums chalk white. I called the closest vet, but when his answer machine picked up I didn't leave a message. There wasn't time to wait for a reply. I then called our regular vet whose clinic was forty-five minutes away but its emergency phone didn't answer either.

Hobson, Tigger, Chocolate, Daisy, and Bungee. Early Morning, December 2001. Last Picture of Bungee. "On Wednesday, December 26th, I recorded in my diary that in putting the dogs out before dinner, 'Bungee not his usual, hyper self.'"

Cursing the fact that emergencies always seem to occur in the wee hours of a Sunday morning, I called our regular vet, Dr. Stafford, at home, and got his voice mail as well. I left a desperate message, "Please, please call me Ron, ASAP. Bungee's dying!"

A half an hour had passed by the time I reached the substitute emergency vet at home. He promised to meet me at clinic in forty-five minutes. I jumped into the car, with Bungee on the seat beside me, panting and looking terrified. As we tore at high speeds over Bozeman pass, the road icy and dangerous, I continued to stroke Bungee, saying, "Hang in there, my boy. Just hang on. We'll have help soon!"

Five blocks from vet's Bungee curled up and seemed more comfortable. His panting stopped. I continued to stroke him, feeling reassured. Two blocks away I felt for his breath but couldn't find it. When we arrived, I got out of car and carried Bungee into the clinic. His body had gone limp and he leaked urine. Rushing in the door, distraught, tears rolling down my cheeks, I shouted, "I can't believe it! Bungee seems dead!"

The emergency vet was new and I did not know him well. He told me he had talked with Stafford who'd advised to spare nothing to save Bungee's life. But he also warned Bungee may have suffered brain damage. Did I really want to take extreme measures? Yes, I pleaded, do everything possible to save him.

The vet looked into Bungee's eyes. "They're fixed and dilated," he said, "It's too late."

I screamed at him, "It can't be! It can't be! Do something." The vet shook his head and put his medical implements away.

"Died of acute liver disease," he said, a diagnosis I still couldn't believe. Even on this last day, Bungee had shown no sign of this ailment. Convinced he had made a misdiagnosis I wondered if, had he correctly identified the problem, he could have saved Bungee. But dazed, I didn't ask. The vet quickly ushered me out the clinic door. I carried Bungee's limp little body and placed it on the seat beside me, then drove home, stroking him and saying over and over, "Bungee, my boy, you cannot be dead. You're too young! Wake up, please, wake up!"

* * * * *

A foot of fresh snow covered the frozen ground when I returned home with Bungee's body. As with Ifrit, he had to wait in the locker freezer until summer for burial. In August, exactly ten years to the day after we'd put Ifrit to rest, we carried him to the cottonwood grove. Posy, who adored her father, accompanied us. Dark clouds signaled the arrival of a fast-moving storm as I hugged and stroked his body.

Wrapping Bungee in a piece of my clothing he'd lain on in my study, I placed him in the grave and tried to make him comfortable. Posy stood by, staring mournfully at her father as I closed the grave. She would not be the same for some time. For a year she would pace the house looking for him. He had been her hero, the alpha dog. But with Daisy getting on in years, that mantle now passed to her, and its weight proved too much. Not knowing how to lead, she nagged her siblings instead, carping at them like a drill sergeant when they stepped out of line.

When Bungee was covered, I knelt next to the loose dirt and whispered goodbye. Never had I felt so close to a dog, nor so bereft, but tears wouldn't come.

23

Cricket

*Do they know, as we do, that their time must come? Yes, they
know. No other way can I interpret those pauses of his latter
life, when, propped on his forefeet, he would sit for long minutes
quite motionless—his head drooped, utterly withdrawn; then turn
those eyes of his and look at me. The look said more plainly than
all words could: "Yes, I know that I must go!"*

> *—John Galsworthy,*
> "Memories," The Inn of Tranquility, *1912*

*Do animals as well as people project themselves? My reply is—
yes; according to my experience they do.*

> *—Elliott O'Donnell,*
> Animal Ghosts, or Animal Hauntings and the
> Hereafter, *1913*

In April, just four months shy of her eighteenth birthday, Panda slipped
into terminal decline. Blind, deaf, and incontinent, she had, despite her
still stout heart, reached the end. I carried her to the porch and held her in
my lap. She licked my face and we talked awhile. Then we drove together
to Dr. Stafford who put her to sleep as I stroked her face and ears. We
buried her under the cottonwoods by Finn, Ifrit, Bungee, and Nobie.

Finn's and Ifrit's last had gone. A humble, quiet little girl who never
complained and never quit. Over her long life, she walked more miles
than any dog we ever knew. We would miss her quiet company, her smile
and her gay, rocking-horse gait.

* * * * *

A month later, just five months after Bungee's death, I completed the
manuscript of *Harvard and the Unabomber* and, at long last, had plenty

Saying Goodbye to Panda, April 30, 2002.
"I carried her to the porch and held her in my lap.
She licked my face and we talked awhile."

of time for hikes. But too late for Bungee. A miracle brought him to me and something equally inexplicable had taken him away. We never learned why. Most experts believe a tumor in the liver ruptured, causing massive internal bleeding. Certainly, a hereditary disease hadn't killed him. His forebears lived to fifteen or more.

Whatever caused his death, Bungee saw it coming. In retrospect, I realized he clung to me passionately because he, as Ifrit had before him, knew the end was near. How was this possible?

Everyone knows dogs have apparent premonitions, but no one knows how they do it. Stories abound of dogs who detect cancer, anticipate epileptic fits and heart attacks, foretell personal calamities, or predict tsunamis or earthquakes. Most animal behaviorists suppose they accomplish these feats not through powers of clairvoyance but rather simply by virtue of their superior senses of smell, observation, and hearing. The cancer or heart attack victim emits a unique odor, they say, or prior to a seizure the dog notices that the epileptic's behavior subtly changes; or before tsunamis and earthquakes, he senses earth vibrations, or gas emissions, or shifts in the earth's electromagnetic field that humans miss.

These suppositions may be correct, but no one can say, for none have been verified by scientific testing. It's not really known how dogs do these things, and the behaviorists' skepticism may just represent philosophical bias. To a man with a hammer, everything looks like a nail; and to such scientists, much of whose education was devoted to training rats to negotiate mazes, dogs are merely stimulus-response machines. These scholars are Cartesians and thus assume animals are simple machines incapable of self-awareness (what scientists call "apperception") or conceiving of the past or future. But in that, at least, they're almost certainly mistaken.

"Ethologists, the scientists who study animal behavior," the *Wall Street Journal* reported recently:

> have amassed thousands of studies showing that animals can count, understand cause and effect, form abstractions, solve problems, use tools and even deceive. But lately scientists have gone a step further: Researchers around the world are providing tantalizing evidence that animals not only learn and remember but that they may also have consciousness—in other words, they may be capable of thinking about their thoughts and knowing that they know.

So dogs may be self-aware and have a concept of the future. But how they might anticipate this future—whether through their senses and powers of reason or though some form of sixth sense—we don't yet know.

That's why critics of these skeptics, such as Cambridge and Harvard educated Rupert Sheldrake, continue to plea for more open-minded scientific study. "I believe we stand on the threshold of a new phase of science," he writes, in which "further research into the powers of nonhuman animals . . . may be able to tell us something very important not only about the nature of life and mind but also about the nature of time."

Indeed, the truth may be found, not in science but philosophy. If dogs are merely stimulus-response machines, they can't be clairvoyant. But if they are thinking beings who possess souls, they may partly live in a dimension that lies beyond time. They would be our windows into the spiritual world and our study of them might reveal, as Sheldrake suggests, more about the nature of time and reality than we ever imagined.

Ifrit's life and death showed me this window, and Bungee's death began to open it for me. Whether he was clairvoyant or not, he could feel pain and contemplate the future. He'd been suffering more than a year; yet like all dogs and especially terriers he had been bred to ignore it. So he remained a Stoic. Unable to tell me, he suffered alone. And this pain, isolation, and prospect of death scared him. Every moment we had together became more precious and he grew afraid to leave my side.

There'd never be another like him. We now knew breeding never recreates the parent. Where, then, did the key to his immortality lie?

Perhaps in a sense the answer did reside in his genes after all—but not, like show dogs, by reducing dogs' genetic diversity, but rather by increasing it. Much of what I loved in Bungee were qualities of his character, which were products of out-crossing. And while none of Bungee's pups exactly resembled him, each shared similarities. Singly, they weren't reproductions but combined they were. Posy inherited his exuberant energy and personality; Hobson and Chocolate his "loyalty gene"; Tigger his joy and love of fishing and his good looks. Bungee left some of himself in each, and together they formed a mosaic that exactly resembled him.

Tigger became my fisher-dog and took Bungee's place on the "A Team." Almost immediately he assumed his father's spot at the foot of my desk. And every day he looked and acted more like his father. While Chocolate still stuck to Diana, Hobson moved closer to me than ever, showering me with fanatic attachment. And when Posy eventually recovered from her grief, she replaced her father's energy and joy in our otherwise sober canine household.

* * * * *

Tigger at Nelson's Spring Creek, August 2004
"Tigger became my fisher-dog and took Bungee's place
on the 'A Team.'"

Alston and Hobson, July 2000
"Hobson moved closer to me than ever, showering
me with fanatic attachment."

In trying to find dogs exactly like Ifrit and Bungee, we had made the same mistake show breeders do who attempt to produce dogs exactly like their foundation stock. Genetic immortality lies not in replication, but diversity—sustaining the health of dogs while simultaneously creating a mosaic or range of resemblances, as Reverend Russell did. He "replicated" Trump, not by producing others exactly like her, but by breeding a loosely defined type that collectively shared family resemblances. And with luck we, too, could do the same thing.

So began our search for Tigger's mate. Now, however, we realized finding a good sporting terrier meant going beyond Montana to hunting communities in the east. And in March I found just such a dog—a short-legged, rough coated JR named, "Chaps." A nationally ranked agility champion, he was featured that month in a Jack Russell calendar. His owners, Dick and Claudette Barker, lived in Florida. I called, and soon through e-mail we became good friends.

Claudette told me that a couple in Vermont named David and Avril Howe, who owned two short, rough-coated females called Ruff and Tumble had already contacted her about breeding one to Chaps.

I called the Howes. English by birth, David and Avril grew up in Devon. As a boy, David had delivered animal feeds to farms around Swimbridge, where Russell had lived many years. Like us, the Howes liked shorter-legged, longer-coated JRs. And also like us, they preferred the sporting type. In November, Avril visited the Barkers, where they bred Ruff to Chaps. In January, the Howes called to say Ruff whelped three pups and they were saving a female for us. Later I flew to Vermont and took the little girl home. We named her, "Truffle."

Long-haired and ten inches tall, plucky, brave, and feminine, Truffle joined the family in March, 2003. Tigger, Hobson, and Chocolate adored her. Formerly inhibited by Bungee's presence, these solemn bachelors had never been playful. But Truffle quickly taught them how to have fun. Within a month they were devising elaborate games—rolling on the floor, playing tug-of-war and running full-out after each other throughout the house.

"The perfect wife for Tigger," Diana said.

We resumed our hikes and walk-rides. Truffle replaced Panda on the Stealth Team and Tigger took Bungee's place on the A Team. The joy of their company melded once again with love of the land as we retraced familiar routes.

* * * * *

On Saturday, February 19, 2005, I woke worrying about Cricket.

"We flew to Vermont and took the little girl home.
We named her 'Truffle.'"

I didn't know why. I'd never seen the dog and hadn't communicated with the Zagrodnicks since we exchanged Christmas cards in December.

Yet, although I never saw Cricket, she held a special place in my heart. She had given me Bungee twelve years earlier, and had endowed him with the traits I loved. For years I'd expected that my travels would eventually take me to Dallas; and when they did, I'd visit Cricket. But they never did, and I'd not thought of her for months until that morning. Overcome with an eerie panic, I thought, "I've got to see her before she dies."

I phoned the Zagrodnicks to suggest I come to see Cricket, but got no answer. From Sunday through Tuesday, I called repeatedly, leaving messages on their voice mail. For some reason, I felt time was critical.

When they didn't reply, I told myself not to worry. They must be on a trip, I decided.

Then Wednesday morning I received an email from Terri. She and John had changed phone service and had new numbers, she explained, so she'd just received my messages. And Cricket, she said, was dead—hit by a car Tuesday afternoon and died later that night. Partially blind and slow afoot, she had been caught under the wheels of a car as it came slowly up their driveway, breaking her pelvis. Terri saw it happen and rushed Cricket to the veterinary hospital. As the vet struggled to save the dog, Terri stayed with her, "telling her," she wrote me, "what happened and that they'd 'have to work through this and that at first it might be difficult,' and she began to shake."

"I immediately laid my hand across her and in stillness said, 'No, it won't be difficult. Everything will be fine.' She stopped shaking. So I believe she did not want to continue . . . Cricket died with her boots on. She did not have, in her old body, the fight that would have been required to recover."

Later, Terri wrote me:

Anyone who knew Cricket knew she was a very special pup, special enough to have been my son and daughter-in-law's flower girl in their wedding. She was decked with a collar of flowers, and on cue came straight from the back door around the house to the path where the guests and I were waiting. She eyed me and came straight to me and jumped in my lap. Great job. We only practiced once.

My shadow.

She had been snake bit—I don't know—maybe four times. Picked up and released by a coyote (I think a car drove by and the coyote dropped her)—that was a close call. She took on a German Shepherd once—the Shepherd won and Cricket never forgot it. She would growl across the lake at his home for the next six years. Of course she and

Maggie [Chocolate's litter mate, whom we sold to the Zagrodnicks] had a couple of run-ins. Maggie had to give in to Cricket, so Cricket won that one. Over the years she's had to have x-rays a couple of times and the vet was always amazed to see the buckshot. I'm sure we have farmer Brown to thank for that, but then he was just protecting his chickens.

There's probably not an inch of my sofa that she hasn't cleaned for me, and if she was in the mood she'd lick your hand for as long as you'd let her. She had the cleanest puppies in the county—three litters.

I loved her more than any dog I've ever owned—she was a gift, never paid a dime for her except for the thousands of dollars in vet bills, but she was worth it all because she was a gift given in love and she knew it.

She died at midnight on a full moon February 22nd, sedated . . . She could have recovered from a broken pelvis except that she, I think, had had enough of recovering and I respect her decision and wish her God speed straight ahead girl. I have a wonderful vet. He had gone up to check on her around 11:30 and knew she was in trouble so he did everything he could. So he was with her. He had treated her for many years. Once he told me, "This dog is gold."

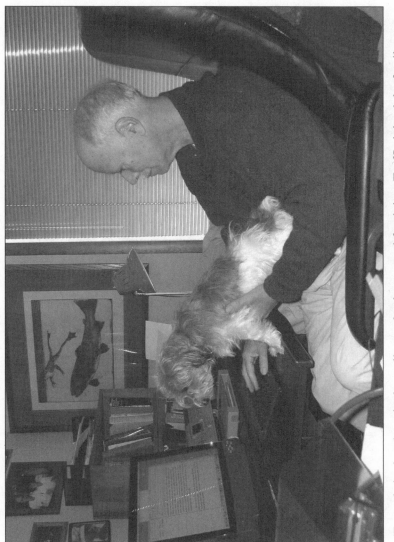

"Long-haired and ten inches tall, spunky, brave, and feminine, Truffle joined the family . . . Tigger, Hobson, and Chocolate adored her."

Truffle, 2003
"The perfect wife for Tigger."

The Stealth Team, July 2003
"Truffle replaced Panda on the Stealth Team."

Posy at Chocolate's Rock, February 2002
"The joy of their company melded once again with the love of
the land as we retraced familiar routes."

24

A Sporting Dog

He was a sporting dog, full of energy, and with undiminished faith in his own powers, in spite of his years . . . he could not endure an inactive life.

> —W. H. Hudson,
> "A Dog in Exile," Idle Days in Patagonia, *1923*

The badger is a desperate fighter, and a much more redoubtable adversary than his neighbour the fox, as nearly every hunter knows to his cost. Many, alas, are the losses of brave and hardy Terriers as a result of encounters with this terrible antagonist.

> —*Pierce O'Conor,*
> Terriers for Sport, *1922*

At first light on March 19th I woke worrying again—this time about Daisy. She had a case of spring fever that wouldn't quit. Although thirteen, she acted three. And that wasn't entirely a good thing. As a sporting terrier, her instincts and energy remained sharply honed and she kept pushing the edge of the envelope. On two occasions in the previous three years, I'd pulled her away from a badger before she got seriously hurt. But I knew she might not always be so lucky.

Spring is every creature's favorite season. Deer, foxes, and many other animals shed their winter coats and drop their young. As the days lengthen, hibernating bears wake and begin munching grass. Ground squirrels and marmots laze in the sun.

Jack Russells love spring as well. Thawing ground releases odors they find irresistible. They go berserk, tearing over the countryside at full race, checking holes in search of quarry. And Daisy was the most fanatic. She never slowed, remaining in a zone no one could penetrate and ignored our calls as she followed scents. Only much later did she reappear, wearing a happy grin. And this spring she was even more wired than usual. There was desperation in her manner, as though she knew she was running out of time and intended to make the most of what remained.

That morning I stood at the glass door facing the south lawn, peering through the gray half-light of dawn. I could hear Diana in the mud room, letting Daisy, Posy, and Tigger out. The dogs yammering, as usual. This was their morning ritual and they loved it. Once free, they'd tear around the house in overdrive, joyfully following Daisy as she checked the yard for wildlife before getting down to the business of making toilet.

Usually it took them about five seconds to run around the house from the mud room door to the south lawn, so I expected to see them appear in front of me at any instant. And sure enough, Posy and Tigger soon zoomed by. But not Daisy. As I stood at the door, I saw Tigger change directions and head for the horse pasture, which he's trained not to do. I ran onto the deck and called, but he ignored me. Instead, he stopped a hundred feet beyond the pasture fence and stared at something small and white on the ground. I ran to him and found Daisy. She lay on her side, barely breathing, with eyes open and unblinking, blood oozing from her mouth.

She'd been outdoors less than two minutes.

* * * * *

Compared with the fox, wrote Geoffrey Sparrow in his 1949 book, *The Terrier's Vocation*, "the badger's bite is often more severe and is under the chin or jaw." No other wound looks quite like it. Daisy apparently spotted the badger the instant she left the house, catching it from behind. A terrible mistake. When a terrier confronts a badger head-on, the sight of its teeth encourages the dog to keep its distance. But if he grabs the badger by the rump, the animal can easily spin around and get a death-grip under the chin before the dog can get free. And while we never saw the badger, that's surely what happened.

I carried Daisy's limp body into the house and called the Bozeman vet on duty, Dr. Waller. By the time we'd made the forty-five minute drive to the hospital, Daisy was in deep shock, her temperature ten degrees below normal. She could breath in, but not out. Something closed her windpipe. One tooth did all the damage. It cut nerves controlling swallowing, nicked the jugular, and crushed the larynx. After six hours of surgery, Daisy still could not swallow.

Waller put her on IV fluids, painkillers, antibiotics, and an anti-inflammatory and checked on her several times throughout the day. At 3:00pm he phoned to say, "she's hanging in there." At 7:00 he called to warn us to expect the worst. She still could not swallow or move her tongue and he hinted she might die at any moment. But she didn't. The next morning he called to say she was improving! She could move her tongue a little and breathe without the machine, although not well. So she might make it. I told him we'd be right over.

But we were too late. As we arrived at the clinic Waller's assistant greeted us to say Daisy died ten minutes earlier. She'd been doing well, was alert and even drinking a bit. Then, with the hospital staff watching she suddenly stiffened and dropped dead of a seizure. Probably, Waller thought, a clot in her damaged jugular had cut off the blood supply to her brain.

* * * * *

Often, the dogs we take for granted tug most at our heartstrings after death. Daisy had disappointed us because she wasn't Ifrit and because she had attacked Panda. Although she couldn't be blamed for either, she sensed our disappointment and couldn't understand. In fact, she was the nearly perfect dog. She spent much of the day on the couch beside my desk and evenings under the pillow between Diana and me. She loved people and was the healthiest dog we'd ever known, neither sick nor lame a day in her life. She was a wonderful mother to her pups. Still fit at thirteen, she showed no sign of age. We expected her to live to eighteen or more.

Why do these little dogs leave such huge holes in our hearts? Diana and I owned fifteen breeds during our lives, and we loved each dog. But none left voids like our little JRs. Why so strong the attachment? Not just because they live longer than most dogs and thus share more years with us. Not just because, thanks to their great genetic diversity their personalities are so different. Not just because they give 100 percent of themselves until they drop. And not just because their incredible bravery makes us not only love but admire them.

When someone asks why we love JRs so much I tell them, "Because they're so much trouble." The more love one puts into a dog or person the more one receives in return. And JRs refuse to be ignored, refuse to be couch potatoes, refuse to be polite and say, "please." They demand, not merely attention, but participation. Other JR owners understand this special, unique bond. "Each and every one of them leaves a void," Terri Zagrodnick wrote us following the deaths of Cricket and Daisy.

John and I were talking last night about the hundreds of Jack Russells that have passed on but that "stand out" over time . . . so many wonderful dogs. Like people, some make their mark and float around in the universe forever. These dogs have evolved to spirit level, I think. Others contribute, and like Daisy sometimes define an era, and then they move on to explore the journey . . .

We are taught how to love through our caring of these little guys and when they pass, we're taught how to let go. Love, and let go. Not a bad lesson to learn. But why are all the really important lessons so hard? I don't like this digging of graves and patting the bodies of friends and putting those first few grains of dirt over their precious bodies. But that is attachment to that which we can see. I'm telling you these dogs teach us so much. We have friends who have a little dog and have decided when she goes there will be no more dogs. It's too painful to lose them! But that's like saying, "I refuse to love again." There is no love without loss . . .

Daisy, in her brave moment of taking on a badger, teaches us about braveness. She teaches us to protect. She teaches us perseverance. And compassion for her struggle to live and her acceptance of her time to go. So in the void left we find that we have to transform our thinking to a much higher level of understanding.

* * * * *

We carried Daisy to the cottonwood grove and buried her next to Bungee. Tigger came to mourn. As I placed her in the grave she seemed asleep. It was difficult to believe she was really gone. She had given us four litters and eighteen pups, including Posy, Hobson, Chocolate, and Tigger. And she tried so hard! Just fifteen pounds and twelve inches tall, she had been the bravest little dog we'd ever known. Like Reverend Russell's favorite terrier, "Tip," she died as she had lived, falling victim to a badger.

It was March 21st, 2005, the vernal equinox. The first day of spring.

Daisy, 1999
"We carried Daisy to the cottonwood grove and buried
her next to Bungee. Tigger came to mourn."

25

Ghosts

There are ghosts that haunt us through life,
There are ghosts that for ever grow,
They roam abroad in the gloaming,
And they are found in the fire's glow.

> —Alys Serrell,
> "Ghosts," Wessex Winnowings, *1925*

Dogs do speak. They speak to us in our dreams. I have met
many men and women who, like me, dream about the dog
they loved who is no more.

> —Roger Grenier,
> The Difficulty of Being a Dog

After Bungee died, his ghost often came to visit. During the day, he'd suddenly be there, sleeping on the sofa or sitting up at my feet, trying to catch my attention. At night, he arrived in Diana's and my dreams, where the settings were always the same: We were in country neither of us had ever been before. We walked up a hill and came to a bright meadow resembling "the beautiful place" Plato described in his account of the afterlife in the myth of Er. Tall, golden grass waved in a stiff breeze. At the end of the meadow, we reached a barnyard. Bungee appeared from behind the barn and greeted us joyously, as though he'd been looking for us.

Finn, Ifrit, Panda, and Daisy sometimes materialized too. Were they really ghosts? After my eerie premonitions of Cricket's and Daisy's deaths, anything seemed possible. Did they suggest something we didn't understand?

Our friends had similar experiences. After Cricket died, Terri Zagrodnick wrote us that:

"After Bungee died, his ghost often came to visit."

Yesterday oddly was my most grievous day. Three days with no Cricket. The pain of that longing to have her was overwhelming until late in the day I heard that unmistakable voice of God saying, "Can you give her to me? Can you? Will you? Will you give her to me?" And I was struck with how much I wanted to yell out, "Mine, mine, mine," even to God. And then I held up my hands and gave her to him not once because once was not sincere but three times until I realized that I had been so blessed to have had her for so many years and that now God wanted to play with her and refresh her. It was his turn. "Would he take good care of her?" I asked. What a silly question.

"I believe my magical Cricket is on her journey," Terri told me a week later, "and is only occasionally looking back to hear me say, 'Go, it's okay . . . go.' There's a very long rope of love between her heart and my heart, amazingly long."

Three weeks later Terri had a dream. "I saw Cricket," she wrote.

From a distance of maybe a hundred feet, I saw her. I was a bit above and she was not at all aware of me. She was prancing through the safest of all forests and she was all clean and lovely with her tail high and her spirits high. She was on a mission. A shaft of light came down through the forest and her beautiful hair was shining. The grass was very green and tall, almost to her shoulders, but her head was high and I could see the wisps of hair trailing from the tips of her ears. She was very, very happy. And that is the beginning of our "new" level of communication.

Terri's friend, Carol Conlee, had a dream about her lost dog, Pirate, the brother of Cricket. When Pirate was three, he disappeared from her yard, apparently kidnapped. Then, after some weeks, he appeared to her in a dream to say he was alive but unhappy. Behind him, Carol noticed a city neighborhood she'd never seen before. She began driving around Dallas looking for that place and after a three-month search found it. She plastered the neighborhood with "stolen dog" posters that displayed Pirate's picture.

A few days later, Carol was sitting on the front steps of her house when a car briefly stopped on the street, its door opened and Pirate jumped out, then the car sped off. Apparently, Carol had seen the kidnappers' neighborhood in her dream, and the posters frightened them into returning the dog.

And Avril Howe had dreams, too. Two years before Bungee died, she had lost a beloved Jack Russell named, "Woofer." Short and rough-coated,

Woofer—whom the Howes nicknamed, "Woogie"—had been Avril's soul mate for fourteen years. At seven Woogie went blind from a disease called lens luxation. Yet she soldiered on, taking daily walks with the Howes, and never leaving Avril's side until cancer took her life.

When Woofer died, she returned to Avril in a dream, as David wrote us, "to lick her tears away."

"Woogie was young again and could see," David went on, "and was very happy and excited, busy having fun and doing doggie things, and she was telling Avril that she was alright and not to worry, and Avril was crying and missing her, and Woofer was all wiggy-waggy and happy and kissing Avril and licking her face, and telling her not to be sad and that she was full of joy and having a wonderful time."

"In our less rational moments," David added, "we hope that we will all be together again one day, and we can imagine Woofer playing together with her friend Bungee . . . and all the other wonderful little creatures past, present, and future."

* * * * *

How irrational was that hope? The folklore of peoples around the world tells of ghost dogs (people who return in the shape of dogs as ghosts), dog ghosts (dogs who become ghosts), dogs that see ghosts, dogs that are afraid of ghosts, dogs who see ghostly things that humans don't, dogs that are clairvoyant, dog ghosts who save lives, people who refuse to enter heaven without their dogs, dogs who project themselves, dogs as psychics, dogs who haunt castles, and spectral hounds.

And some of these stories are reportedly true. In 1935, Cecil Aldin, an artist famed for his loving depiction of dogs and other animals left his beloved bull terrier, Cracker, at his cottage in Majorca, Spain, where he had been living, to return to his native England for a visit. But, while in England, Aldin died unexpectedly. According to his biographer, Roy Heron, "At the very time Cecil Aldin breathed his last at the London Clinic, Cracker, 1,000 miles away, set up a heart-rending howl such as he had never made before and could not be quietened. Nor for many hours did news of Aldin's death arrive. The incident was confirmed by (his wife) Rita Aldin, who said there was no way the dog could have known anything was amiss, except by some canine sixth sense."

Countless other individuals, many prominent like Aldin, swear to having been visited by their dog after death. One was the wife of John Galsworthy, author of *The Forsyte Saga*, following the premature death of their spaniel, Chris, at age five in 1911. "He has once come back," Galsworthy writes, describing his wife's experience:

> It was Old Year's Night, and she was sad, when he came to her in visible shape of his black body, passing round the dining-table from the window-end, to his proper place beneath the table, at her feet. She saw him quite clearly; she heard the padding tap-tap of his paws and very toe-nails; she felt his warmth brushing hard against the front of her skirt. She thought then that he would settle down upon her feet, but something disturbed him, and he stood pausing, pressed against her, then moved out towards where I generally sit, but was not sitting that night. She saw him stand there, as if considering; then at some sound or laugh, she became self-conscious, and slowly, very slowly, he was no longer there. Had he some message, some counsel to give, something he would say, that last night of the last year of all those he had watched over us? Will he come back again?

John Neihardt, author of *Black Elk Speaks,* reportedly had a similar visit from his dead dog. According to ethnologists Randy Russell and Janet Barnett,

> Neihardt and his wife had been involved in a minor car accident and were visited shortly thereafter by their insurance agent. All three were seated at the dining-room table while the agent took notes on the incident. Suddenly he said, "I'm sorry, but your dog is making me nervous. Would you mind putting him out? Startled, the Neihardts asked, "Dog? What dog are you talking about?" "Why you know," replied the agent, "the little black Spaniel that's under the table." He bent to peer below the table, then shrugged, "Well, he's not there now. He slipped out, so never mind." The Neihardts exchanged glances but let the topic drop. What they didn't tell the agent was that only a week before, their beloved black Spaniel had died of old age.

It's not surprising then, that according to a 2002 ABC News opinion poll, 90 percent of respondents believe in the existence of heaven where people live forever with God after they die and 43 percent think their pets will go there too.

So the question we first asked after Phineas died remained unanswered. Do we really lose them or do they—and we—continue on somehow and somewhere after death, as Terri suggested? Had we really seen Bungee's ghost, or had a dream or memory just transported us back in time?

Or were ghosts, dreams, and memories all the same thing?

26

Eternity

To us believing physicists the distinction between past, present and future (i.e., between what is now and what is not now) has only the significance of a stubborn illusion.

> —*Albert Einstein,*
> Quoted from A World without Time, *by Paul Yourgrau*

In traditional quantum cosmology, there is no time at the most basic physical level.

> —*Frank J. Tipler,*
> The Physics of Immortality

Six months after Daisy died, Diana and I took our annual walk-ride to the Divide. She rode her Morgan filly, Antigone, and I followed on foot with Posy and Tigger—the now abbreviated "A Team."

We began near our house and climbed thousands of feet to the cold and windy pass surrounded by the rock-covered peaks that mark the boundary between the Yellowstone and Boulder River watersheds. At these higher elevations, the trail is rarely used; and the only visible signs of change along it are the Douglas fir and lodgepole pine felled by avalanches and wind storms during previous winters.

The trail took us past places, which, like Nobie's Rock, had been named after the dog who left his imprint there—spots like Panda's Rock, where she loved to perch and enjoy the view; the Blue Spring, which we renamed Bungee's Spring, where he and I so often sat on a log side by side, enjoying each other's company; and Daisy's Dip, the stream pool hidden among deadfall that she discovered one hot July day years ago.

Halfway up we came to an open alpine meadow surrounded by vertical rock peaks which formed a gigantic amphitheater. Then we proceeded up grueling switchbacks, where the dogs quenched their thirst in rivulets of melted snow, and ultimately to the divide itself, to huddle in the wind, suck in the thin air and enjoy the view before retracing our steps a short distance to the tree line below, where, under the protective canopy of white bark pine, we lay on the sparse grass and shared our lunches with the dogs.

The trek took on the aspect of a voyage through time. When one visits a place after an absence and finds nothing changed, every step recalls a memory. It's like returning to the home where we grew up to find everything exactly as it was: the Hudson Super-Six Station Wagon still parked in the driveway, the triptych above the mantle, the odor of cornbread wafting in from the kitchen. And when we climb the stairs and enter our bedroom, we find our old Erector set still there, parts strewn across the floor as we'd left them sixty years earlier.

And on this trip especially, every place stirred a memory, as though the very rocks held the spirits of our departed dogs. What if, I wondered as I slogged up the trail behind Diana and Antigone that morning, time really doesn't exist? The mysteries of immortality and premonitions of death both concern time: whether Bungee continues to live *after* death, and how I could have anticipated Cricket's and Daisy's *before* they died. If there's no "before" or "after," if everything in the universe exists "under the aspect of eternity" as Spinoza said, then the puzzlement disappears. Immortality's impossible only if time is real. If it isn't, immortality isn't just possible, but *necessary*.

Without time, there's no "before" or "after"; and moving backward would be as easy as moving forward. There would be no difference between ghosts (i.e., what once lived) and memories (what still lives in imagination). If time's not real, then everything that ever existed *always* exists. The English poet, William Wordsworth understood this. In "Intimations of Immortality," written in 1806, he wrote:

> What though the radiance which was once so bright
> Be now for ever taken from my sight,
> Though nothing can bring back the hour
> Of splendour in the grass, of glory in the flower;
> We will grieve not, but rather find
> Strength in what remains behind;
> In their primal sympathy
> Which having been must ever be;
> In the soothing thoughts that spring
> Out of human suffering;
> In the faith that looks through death,
> In years that bring the philosophic mind.

Alston and the "Dynamic Duo" at Davis Creek Divide
"The trek took on the aspect of a voyage through time."

If time does not exist, then that "which having been must ever be." But time *is* real, isn't it? The idealists were mistaken, weren't they? Most modern philosophers still think they had been mistaken. But today physicists aren't so sure.

* * * * *

While a graduate student at Princeton in the 1960s I had lived just around the corner from a mathematician named Kurt Gödel. A refugee from Nazi Germany, Gödel was a fellow at the prestigious Institute for Advanced Study. And while few knew it then, he had already proved the idealists right.

In 1931 Gödel published a mathematical theorem that came to be known among scholars as the "incompleteness theorem" and among the wider public as "Gödel's Proof," which earned him a reputation as perhaps the greatest mathematician who ever lived. In it, he showed why the objects of mathematics, such as numbers, must be indeed, real, abstract, and unchanging—just as the idealists had been saying all along. But he wasn't finished. In 1949 he published another paper that showed how Einstein's famous theory of relativity, which is widely regarded as being true, entails that *time does not exist*.

Einstein had been aware that the unreality of time was an implication of his theory. But he thought the idea so bizarre he refused to accept it. If relativity suggests time is not real, then, he had supposed, there must be a bug in his theory somewhere.

Gödel showed there was no bug.

Unfortunately, Gödel's work had been so revolutionary that most mathematicians, physicists, and philosophers at the time didn't understand its implications. Certainly I didn't, even though I was studying with Gödel's colleagues and serving as assistant instructor in a graduate-level course devoted to the mathematics Godel had developed in his incompleteness theorem called "recursive functions."

Even today most philosophers remain blind to the stunning significance of Gödel's work. But recently many physicists, at least, have been catching on. For his insight that time isn't real has helped inspire countless new theories about the nature of time and the universe, which imply various ways to think about eternity and immortality. Some physicists note that if time doesn't exist, then time travel may be possible—perhaps by passing through "worm holes" in the cosmos that link one period with another. Others suppose there are many worlds running in parallel time, each differing only infinitesimally from another, so that, for instance, a dog that dies in one world may still be alive in another.

＊ ＊ ＊ ＊ ＊

As we continued our descent from the divide, I thought of Phineas and the twenty-seven year search for the immortality of dogs his death inspired and how this pursuit now led us back to the beginning, to questions about time. And it seemed to prove Rupert Sheldrake right, that animals may not only reveal to us the nature of life, but of time as well. Ifrit and Bungee and the other dogs we loved showed us a universe where time does not exist and where—however fragile and short-lived their bodies may have been—their spirits never die.

At Bungee's Spring we stopped to rest. I sat on a log as Diana tethered Antigone to a willow branch then sat beside me.

"Do you think Bungee could squeeze through a worm hole?" I asked.

"Why not?" she answered as Posy jumped into her lap. "He's a terrier, isn't he? Squeezing through holes is what terriers do."

"As we continued our descent from the Divide,
I thought of Phineas and the twenty-seven year search for the
immortality of dogs his death inspired."

27

Millegan Return

Stand still, you ever-moving spheres of Heaven,
That time may cease, and midnight never come.

> —*Christopher Marlowe,*
> The Tragical History of Doctor Faustus, *1604*

Time the destroyer is time the preserver.

> —*T. S. Eliot,*
> *"The Dry Salvages," 1941*

The road was even worse than I remembered it, which was a good sign. Ignoring my steering efforts, the pickup lurched from one set of ruts to another, as Avril Howe sat beside me, enjoying the scenery. Truffle stood on my lap, paws on the steering wheel, eyes glued on the road ahead. "Pretending she's driving," I thought. Chocolate occupied his usual perch—the arm rest between the front seats—keeping an eye out for jaywalking gophers. Hobson hid under his pillow in the back seat, as usual. David Howe and Diana followed behind us in the Howe's Subaru, carrying their three JRs, Ruff, Tumble, and Truffle's sister, Pickle.

Our route followed Rock Creek, as the tiny serpentine stream ducked through thickets of willow and past hillside stands of aspen, shimmering in the late summer sun. Four decades ago, beaver had consumed all this vegetation along the creek, leaving the stream barren as a ditch. Now, it once more grew in profusion and beaver had returned. The cycle of nature continued.

We passed an abandoned house, nearly invisible in deep shadow. On a bare knoll above the house, we could see the shell of a one-room school; its white paint turned lead grey, its windows broken, and its cupola missing. A sign in front of the house said, "No Hunting. No Fishing. Don't Ask."

"This was Lingshire," I told Avril, anticipating her question. "Used to be quite a community here—dances in the schoolhouse every Saturday night, everything. Then Wellington Rankin, who was then the biggest landowner in Montana, bought everybody out and hired ex-convicts as ranch hands. Lingshire earned a reputation as a tough place, and the town died. "When we came, only Rankin's foreman, who everyone called 'Pap,' remained. I used to visit Pap and talk about the old days. But he died thirty years ago."

Beyond Lingshire, we left the trees behind and passed through rolling, open rangeland. No sign of humans anywhere. "This is what Montanans call, 'big country,'" I said, as much to myself as to Avril. Grass, bleached gold by the August sun, undulated with the wind as our route climbed higher into the mountains. Near the top of Gaddis Hill, we came to the abandon farmhouse the dogs and I had so often hiked by more than two decades ago.

On the other side of Gaddis, we reentered forest and the road dropped steeply, carving hairpin switchbacks through the pines. On the horizon we caught glimpses of the Big Belt Mountains—pastel layers of gold, green, and purple merging with the sky.

Halfway down we stopped at a ranch gate. "This is it," I said. "This is where it all began."

* * * * *

The new owner's son greeted us warmly when we arrived as the ranch buildings. "We won't be long," I told him. "We just want to show the Howes our old place."

The new owners clearly loved the ranch, and it showed. Their large family spent much time there and they took good care of the land. But little of the old remained. The buildings had undergone a near total transformation. Few signs indicated that Diana and I—or Ben Dunn and the Copes before us—had ever lived there.

Beautifully and conscientiously kept, the buildings shined with the care of money. A new roof we wanted but couldn't afford covered the barn. The granary had become a lovely guest cabin. Bunkhouses replaced both the Cat House where Zoomie and Mumtazi once slept and The Manse, where we'd slept with Una, Finn, Ifrit, and a vibrant community of packrats. The kitchen and bath houses, that we had built with Charley Reissing, were gone as well. In their place stood a lodge more suitable for accommodating the new owner's large family and their guests. The pasture fences and corrals were gone, along with the cattle and horses. Only the Hobby House remained.

"The Manse," I explained to David and Avril, "stood there. And just beyond it, our vegetable garden. And see the old tree on the far side of the meadow? That's where we buried Mumtazi."

Hiking to the point, our little party of four people and six terriers followed the same wagon ruts Diana and I had taken so many evenings with Una, Phineas, Little Orphan Annie, Finn, and Ifrit.

The dead tree overhanging the lip of the canyon still stood where David and I had gazed at the river in 1972 and he had exclaimed, "This is it!" David is middle aged now and has a grown son, but the magnificent canyon remained just as it was. The sheer limestone cliffs still shimmered red and gold, and, a thousand feet below, the river still meandered through fields of bleached grass. Stands of aspen decorated the river's banks. Suicide Trail, which Ravelin and I had blazed and where Una and I had often hiked into the solitude of the canyon, was overgrown and impassible. No one had used it since we left.

* * * * *

At noon, we hiked the Packdown into the canyon. Rarely used now, this ancient Indian route had nearly disappeared as grasses reclaimed their long-lost territory. Otherwise, every pebble under our feet seemed as it was in 1972 when our family scampered down the trail for the first time.

Halfway to the river the trail crossed a bare ridge and we could see Bud and Annie Laurie's ranch below. Just beyond the corral lay the bluff where their predecessor, Jack Ramsey, fell to his death accidentally backing his wagon team of horses off it. Bud and Annie Laurie are gone and their cabin had burned to the ground a few years ago. The ranch now belongs to a corporation executive who's building a trophy house there.

The afternoon light reflected off the cliffs that framed the meadow as we emerged from the woods at the bottom of the Packdown and walked towards the river. We were alone in this great amphitheater, and our words seemed to echo off the canyon walls. Sitting on the bank, we ate lunch and talked about the future of Millegan and Jack Russells as we watched the dogs play in the water. Shifting gravel carried by floods had changed the river bottom, creating new pools and filling the one where our boys had bungeed.

But something was wrong. While the beauty around us remained undiminished, the people were gone and much of the land surrounding our old ranch was in trouble.

Since leaving Millegan, I had visited wildlife preserves throughout the world. I hiked hundreds of miles in many national parks but never

"The dead tree overhanging the lip of the canyon still stood where David and I had gazed at the river below in 1972 and he exclaimed, 'This is it.'"

encountered the diversity of life we had found by the Smith. This abundance was a product of the people born and buried here. They kept a community that breathed life into the land.

As they departed and died, these Milleganers or their heirs sold to celebrities, investment bankers, and scions of famous families who use the ranches as summer retreats. Although less itinerant than their counterparts in Paradise Valley –and hence not yet sparking subdivision sprawl—these newcomers' effects on the fisheries and land are otherwise similar.

They give generously to preservation groups which publicize the Smith River heavily by taking wealthy contributors down it on fund-raising trips. These guests then return on their own with commercial guides, or bring friends, turning the river into a summertime superhighway for upscale recreation. Now, according to Montana's Department of Fish, Wildlife and Parks, 10,000 fisherman cast their lines at trout on the Smith each summer.

And although well intentioned, many of these newcomers would preserve Millegan Country like a moth in formaldehyde. Not knowing that by burning and hunting, Indians had kept the range healthy and game numbers in balance; that by irrigating fields and raising livestock, homesteaders had stimulated grass growth and improved wildlife habitat; and not realizing that to preserve the landscape, they must do likewise, they visited just a few weeks a year to "ranch the view" then locked the gates and left.

Millegan had become a museum, filled with carefully protected but decaying treasures. Along the Smith and by Millegan Road that day, the telltale signs of this neglect were evident: the eerie absence of livestock, dying grasses, soil erosion, and barren stands of pine shading out the edible forbs, berries, and deciduous trees on which browsing animals depend. The Smith's monster trout I once had found so numerous were gone, victims of the thousands of anglers who float the Smith each summer and the silt from soil erosion that smothers their eggs.

* * * * *

So today Millegan Country leads a double life. In summer, it is loved with a destroying passion by corporate CEOs, trust fund legatees, and countless expeditioners; while the rest of the year it stands empty and mute—a victim, both seasons, of the slow death of rural America. The people of Millegan, the Blackfoot and early ranchers, intended to stay forever. Their resolve made them good stewards. But, like our family, they eventually had to leave and the signs of their sojourn gradually

Tigger in the Smith River
"We watched the dogs play in the water."

"Near the path we found Scott Allen's cabin, half buried in silt by the flood of 1981. The earth was slowly reclaiming his legacy."

disappeared. Like Jack Russells, they became casualties of an economy which no longer has use for those who live on the land.

But while we watched the dogs play in the water that afternoon, it seemed these earlier land stewards had never really left. Their spirits remained. As part of the history of Millegan, they will stay forever. Once having lived here, they always live here. So we too, along with our dogs and other animals, will be embedded together in the land for eternity.

Diana and I had been mistaken all along. We'd never really needed to mourn leaving the ranch or to embark on a quixotic quest for our dogs' immortality. They were already ours forever. Over more than twenty years we'd lived with a sense of loss—of the ranch and of our dogs. Somehow these sadnesses had fused in our hearts. The two pains became one. But we'd really never lost them. Each *having been, must ever be.* That we once lived here remains a fact and will forever. And we didn't need Plato or Einstein to prove dogs never die. For, having once lived, they always will. They—or their ghosts—keep us company until we die and beyond.

Everything passes and everything endures. The shadows hung like curtains across the field as we headed home. I did not want to leave. Near the path we found Scott Allen's cabin, half buried in silt by the flood of 1981. The earth was slowly reclaiming his legacy. Scott had been gone for more than twenty years, but his pots and pans stood by the stove, as though he had just stepped outside for a minute.

Epilogue

The Future of Dogs

The delight I experienced in my communings with
Nature did not pass away, leaving nothing but a recollection
of vanished happiness to intensify a present pain. The
happiness was never lost, but...had a cumulative effect on
the mind and was mine again.

> —W. H. Hudson,
> Far Away and Long Ago, *1918*

Then some, who through this garden pass,
When we two, like thyself, are clay,
Shall see thy grave upon the grass,
And stop before the stone, and say:

People who lived here long ago
Did by this stone, it seems, intend
To name for future times to know
The dachshound, Geist, their little friend

> —Matthew Arnold,
> *"Geist's Grave," 1881*

I'm shivering in bed with the covers over my head, thinking, "Why doesn't Diana close the window?"

It's November, pitch dark, wind's up, and the temperature's flirting with zero. But she believes in fresh air. Lots of it. Thank goodness I have three furry hot water bottles to ward off hypothermia: Hobson's warm body's presses against my chest; Chocolate, lying on "Felix," the stuffed pillow between Diana and me that resembles a raccoon, mashes his cheek on mine; and Truffle, deep undercover, licks my left foot.

At last Diana stirs, and I clamp my eyes tightly shut, pretending to sleep. It's her turn to get up first—always is. She tiptoes out of the bedroom and down the hall. In a minute, I hear the kitchen door open and know she's letting our Irish Wolfhound, Grizelle, out. The newest member of our family, Grizelle does her toilet more quickly than a soldier in combat, so I count to fifteen and calculate she's done and back in the kitchen again, and Diana's about to let the Dynamic Duo (Posy and Tigger) out. They're not as efficient as Grizelle but harder to ignore. They know I'm in the bedroom with the Stealth Team and don't like it one bit. So they park themselves outside our window and howl. When they begin, the Stealthers explode from under the covers and throw themselves against the window. Cacophony reigns.

Deciding it's time to get up, I shuffle to the mud room and let Posy and Tigger in, then shuffle back to the bedroom. Standing aside for safety, I open the door. The three Stealthers explode through it, snarling and biting like dueling pit bulls. Hobson dashes for the north door, dragging Truffle, who has got him by the neck, and Chocolate, who's gnawing on his left thigh.

I get dressed, then bring up wood from the basement, start the fire in the stove, let the Stealthers in again, and enjoy breakfast and the morning paper with Diana. After the meal, I cycle the Stealthers out and indoors a second time, leaving Hobson and Truffle in my study (making sure the baby gate is shut) and Chocolate in the bedroom. Then I cycle the Dynamic Duo a second time. Once back in, they explode down the hall. Tigger throws himself against the bedroom door to get at Chocolate, who's on the other side ripping up the wall-to-wall carpeting in a fury. Posy rockets past and charges the baby gate.

Unfortunately, I hadn't quite latched that door and when Posy stuck her nose through the gate, the door opens; and Truffle, lurking on the other side, latches onto Posy's nose and won't let go. Posy screams in panic as Truffle, snarling, shakes her victim as though she were killing a gopher. I put on heavy leather gloves and pry Truffle's jaw open. And it turns out she hasn't even broken Posy's skin. They were just "getting re-acquainted" it seems.

After six hours at work in my study with Tigger, Hobson, and Truffle, I leave on a hike with the Stealth Team. The snow is deep and hard going. On the way to Nobie's Rock, the dogs see a moose. It is a large cow moose, perhaps 1,200 pounds. She's standing on the other side of the barbed wire fence that delineates the National Forest boundary. She's too tempting a target for the JRs to resist. Quickly, they improvise a game, dashing under the fence to nip the moose's fetlocks, then scampering back inside the forest boundary when she tries to stomp them to death. The dogs are enjoying themselves immensely, confident they're safe behind the fence. They don't know it wouldn't even slow the moose down.

Eventually, I am able to gather the dogs on leashes. They're happy and pleased with themselves. It was the most fun they'd had since last fall when they were sprayed by a skunk.

Another day draws to a close. In the evening, we read in bed with Grizelle and the JRs spread around us—Posy, Chocolate, and Tigger tethered to their nests for the sake of household peace.

"Thank God," I say to myself. "Life has returned to normal."

* * * * *

The answers to Kipling's question came, not with a sudden rush but through thirty year's dawning. When Phineas died, we embarked on a search to see if he might survive death. Our desire to believe in their immortality intensified as we lost, one by one, Nobie, Ifrit, Finn, Bungee, Panda, and Daisy. We thought that if we knew they hadn't really died, they wouldn't still tear our hearts so; and the sting of loss would fade.

At first, we sought to ensure their "genetic immortality" through breeding, but this inevitably failed. Inbreeding, as practiced by the purebred industry, leads not to genetic immortality but to genetic death. And out-crossing, while producing healthier results, does so by promoting diversity, not replication.

Eventually we realized the answer to Kipling had lain at our feet all along. Every day our dogs show us another reason why we give them our hearts. And all these reasons spring from the same source. We love them because they embody the triumph of spirit over mortality. And being spirits, they never die. It is through the window of their brief lives that we glimpse eternity.

And it is the land that draws and holds us together. For thousands of years, our ancestors and we shared their company on the land, forging bonds that, being spiritual, survive death. And since it is their spirits we love, only love gives us eyes to see their spirits.

I still miss the dogs who passed on. But now the memories evoke not grief but gratitude. They gave us love and taught us the meaning of life, death, and immortality. What could be greater gifts than that?

"In the fall of 2006 we bred Truffle to Tigger."

"And they produced four lovely pups—Thumper, Flower, Pansy, and Clover."

"Thumper, Cricket's great-grandson, has gone to live with Cricket's family—the Zagrodnicks—in Dallas."

Still, I'm looking for ways to keep Bungee and Daisy's line going. Their children are getting on in years now: Posy's thirteen, Hobson twelve, Chocolate nine, and Tigger nearly seven. In the fall of 2006 we bred Tigger and Truffle, and they produced four lovely pups—Thumper, Flower, Pansy, and Clover. Thumper, Cricket's great-grandson, has gone to live with Cricket's family—the Zagrodnicks—in Dallas. Pansy's now in Florida with the Barkers and her grandfather, Chaps. Flower and Clover are staying with us. Originally, we intended to keep just Flower, but Clover, courageous and vulnerable, born blind in one eye due to a neo-natal accident, took my heart and wouldn't let go.

Diana asks why we're keeping any pups at all, as we'll be in our mid-eighties before Flower and Clover die—even if we're lucky enough to live that long. I reply that "I don't want to run out of JRs."

*　*　*　*　*

While I mourn our dogs less now, I fret over the future of dogs and the land more. For the global assault on rural communities has reached "the last best place," as Montanans call our state, leaving dogs nowhere to go.

On the trails around Paradise Valley we encounter more hikers—people with big city faces wearing L.L.Bean jackets and carrying GPS receivers who stare through us like New Yorkers avoiding eye contact on the subway. Super rich, bi-coastal CEOs and trust fund cowboys continue to buy out the local ranchers; build million dollar homes; stay an average of three weeks a year; and, after two or three years when the novelty wears off, move on to Santa Fe or Jackson.

In England, the anti-rural sports lobby has achieved total victory. In February 2006 it outlawed fox hunting, and even forbade the use of dogs to kill anything but mice and rats. But this new law hasn't spared animal lives, prevented unnecessary cruelty, or protected nature. Government agents still gas thousands of badgers annually, yet the animals remain as numerous as ever and still pose a health threat to cattle. The ban on hunting fox hasn't increased the numbers of these animals, which were never at risk in the first place. Rather it merely ensures that government agents and licensed private individuals now do the killing, using guns and lethal traps.

Analogous cultural changes threaten sporting dogs in America. While hunting traditions are stronger here than in England, public understanding of the sport continues to decline as the urbanization of public values continues.

"Pansy's now in Florida with the Barkers and her grandfather, Chaps"

Flower at Nine Weeks
"Flower and Clover are staying with us."

Clover at Twelve Weeks

"Clover, courageous and vulnerable, born blind in one eye due to a neonatal accident, took my heart and wouldn't let go."

* * * * *

While many purebred dog breeders take great care not to breed too closely or propagate inherited diseases and a few still prize performance over conformation, on the whole purebred breeding has become a juggernaut whose practices threaten the future of the animal. More than forty-two million pedigreed dogs are now kept as pets; the number of national AKC dog shows grew from one (Westminster) in 2000 to nine in 2006 alone, while those who attended spent collectively $330 million. To be sure, a few breeder associations—particularly those representing sporting or working dogs such as retrievers, pointers, guard, and sheep dogs—still stress performance over conformation and, like Alisa Crawford's JRTCA, endorse the policy of "Just say 'no' to the AKC." But this has not prevented the larger organization from establishing competing registries of these same breeds where studbooks are closed and dogs are judged on conformation, not performance.

And that spells trouble.

* * * * *

"The standard is the blueprint for the breed," papillon breeder Charlotte McGowan explained on PBS' February 4, 2004 NOVA program, "Dogs and More Dogs."

"In this particular breed," Ms. McGowan continued:

the ears are very important; they're set at a 45 degree angle to the head . . . they're round, like this, and they're fringed. The skull end is two-thirds, the stop is defined, the nose is tapered, the eyes are round. These are all the elements that go into making a perfect papillon.

"We really enjoy the ability to take the gene pool and use it like paints," she explained. "It's our art. That is my art. I made this beautiful dog that I enjoy. I made her—I chose her sire and her dam, I chose several generations to make this beautiful dog. I'm very proud of her.

Her mother was bred to her mother's grandson to produce her. And when I choose a mate for her, I'm going to choose her grandfather who was also her great grandfather. The reason I do the close breeding is that I have something very good. I want to keep what I have and I want to improve it. And by closing down the number of potential genes, I'm going to improve my chances of doing that.

Alston, Truffle, and Hobson, May 2005
"Whatever the future may bring, the present and past
are full of riches."

Tigger at Panda's Rock, November 2006
"Each day, when I trek into the mountains with the 'Dynamic Duo' or
'Stealth Team,' the spirits of Phineas, Finn, Ifrit, Nobie, Panda, Bungee,
and Daisy keep me company."

The NOVA narrator notes, "Charlotte Mcgowan has been able to avoid the pitfalls of inbreeding her papillons. But hundreds of thousands of other purebred dogs are suffering from genetic diseases." And, indeed, they are. The purebred business has become a virtual industry, not only in the production of disease but in the creation of misfits as well. As biologist Coppinger explains, breeders "select for the exaggerated form. They select for the really big ones. They select for the flattest face. They select for the longest face. The breeds wind up with weird conformations. Each breed takes on an unnatural shape, becoming a freak of nature."

Consider what Keith Steward Thomson, former President of the Academy of Natural Sciences writing in 1996, says they've done to the bulldog:

> There is an almost voyeuristic fascination in the physical deformities that have been bred into the modern bulldog—the severely brachyce-phalic head, prognathous upcurved mandible, distorted ears and tail. A modern bulldog . . . more resembles a veterinary rehabilitation project than a proud symbol of athletic strength or national resolve. Not only is this dog grotesquely disfigured, it is partially handicapped by the insult to its nasal and respiratory apparatus. Furthermore, bulldog pups have to be delivered by Caesarian section.

How did this happen? "The answer," Thomson writes,

> is fashion and breeding for fashion. One only has to compare the English bulldog of 1996 with that of 1840 to see how fashion rein-forced or, perhaps, led by those arbiters of canine conformation—the various kennel clubs—has changed this dog. . . . in truth, the dog is cruelly malformed.

But the bulldog is just one of fashion breeding's victims. Borzoi pups' noses have been bred so long that some have difficulty suckling their mother's teat. The sloping backs and angulated hocks of today's German Shepherds must contribute to, or aggravate, the hip dysphasia that has become epidemic in the breed. Sealyhams are too large and fox terriers too tall for underground work. And, in our experience, the once lovely Mastiff and Great Dane have become medical basket cases. According to Coppinger, "Lord Tweedmouth [who created the golden retriever] had good dogs because he had a good breeding program that included a high percentage of crossbreeding . . . today's household golden retriever is a caricature of Lord Tweedsmouth's dogs."

Pathologist George A. Padgett has identified 532 inherited diseases afflicting purebred dogs. Over two-thirds of Newfoundlands are born with a genetic defect, he says, as are 40.3 percent of cairn terriers, 29.8 percent of bichon frise, and 33.5 percent of Scotties. Thirty percent of Dalmations are born deaf. Many Norwich terriers and Boston terriers can only be whelped by Cesarean section.

Most breeders, writes Padgett, hide the severity of the problem from themselves and others by keeping closed registries—i.e., listing only healthy dogs in pedigrees and not those born defective—and failing to keep pedigrees that note diseases in a dog's ancestry. (He calls this the "only talk about the good dog" syndrome.) This form of self-deception is, he says, a "serious problem" made worse by the belief among breeders that any dog that wins in the show ring is "breedable"—a practice that he says is "just plain dumb. No. It's not dumb, it's *stupid!*"

Compounding this folly are the breeding of what Padgett calls "matadors"—those show ring champions that "produce large numbers, perhaps hundreds or even thousands of offspring."

This spread of genetic diseases has gone so far that it will take many years to reverse. Nor, moreover, are all the ailments physical. Some are psychological. According to Karen Overall, a scientist at the University of Pennsylvania studying the links between inbreeding and behavior who was interviewed on the NOVA show, among these ailments is something akin to autism. "Dogs who are anxious and withdraw from people," she explains, "are just like a lot of schizophrenic and autistic humans who withdraw from people and can't interact."

Yet, so far, few professional breeders have taken even the first steps to reforming their business. What must be done, says Padgett, is for breeders to keep open registries and pedigrees that reveal the defects of a pup's ancestors, then to "dilute" the defective genes by breeding only to dogs lacking it. But most professional breeders don't take these steps and the few efforts to introduce healthy genes into a breed population face such fierce breeder resistance that they're soon abandoned.

* * * * *

What does the future hold?

Biologists sometimes refer to animals such as peregrine falcons, grizzly bears, and northern spotted owls as "indicator species." By this they mean that the decline of these animals indicates the entire biological communities of which they are members are at risk. So too, Jack Rus-

"Their graves lie hidden beside a small stream, surrounded by a nearly impenetrable, densely-packed stand of aspen. Huge cottonwoods tower of them."

sells are an indicator species. As they go, so will all dogs. And the Jack Russell's future does not look good.

While most terrier breeds succumbed to closed studbooks and rigid conformation standards many decades ago, the little JR remained a pure sporting dog until the 1980s. But now its transformation into a show breed has begun as well. The "acceptance by the masses" that *Sports Illustrated* feared twenty-seven years ago has come to pass, and already we see the consequences of this attention: the transformation of the Jack Russell into spidery "Parson Russells" that all look the same. Inbreeding is widespread. Blencathra Badger, a show Parson Russell that won Best of Breed at the 1991 Crufts (England) Dog Show, sired 174 pups in America alone and another 79 since returning to the UK and has been touted to have had "no foreign blood (in his line) for fourteen generations." Not surprisingly, given this trend, genetically transmitted diseases that had once been rare among Jack Russells are showing up more frequently. And if the JR succumbs, can any sporting dog survive?

* * * * *

Whatever the future may bring, the present and past are full of riches. Each day; winter and summer; rain, snow, or shine; when I trek into the mountains with the Dynamic Duo or Stealth Team, the spirits of Phineas, Finn, Ifrit, Nobie, Panda, Bungee, and Daisy keep me company. I take delight in watching Bungee lead the way with his joyous, hip-hop skipity-step canter; Nobie nervously scanning the sky for possible thunderstorms; Panda effortlessly motoring along like the Energizer Bunny; Daisy, a gleam of pure joy in her eyes, showing Hobson her favorite badger holes; Phineas leaping over the tall grass in search of gophers; dour Finn, stubby tail in air, combing rocks for marmots; and gentle Ifrit by my side, looking up at me with a love that could melt rock.

And occasionally, in the evenings, I visit the grove where all but Phineas now lie—no longer to mourn but to give thanks. I sit on the ground and brush the leaves off their head stones and take solace in the thought that, in a deeper reality, we remain together.

Their graves lie hidden beside a small stream, surrounded by a nearly impenetrable, densely packed stand of aspen. Huge cottonwoods tower over them, blocking the sun and making the cemetery resemble a small grotto. Suckers of aspen—tiny shoots of new trees that sprout from the stand's prodigious and ancient root system—crowd the ground claiming every inch of free space and threatening to close the narrow entrance.

In the fall, a thick carpet of newly fallen leaves covers the ground. In the spring, grasses, fed by the stream, reach three feet or more. So keeping this little space open and head stones visible requires constant tending—to cut back aspen limbs, rake leaves, mow grass and suckers, and collect the dead branches dropped by the cotton-woods. If I were to cease grooming for just one season, the graves would disappear.

And that's part of the plan: After we're gone, no one will know we are here.

End

Image Information and Credits

Frontispiece: "Bungee," photo of portrait of Bungee painted by Margaret Merry for the author. (p. ii)

"Alston with Panda and Ifrit, 1987," photo by Michael J. Sachell, with permission. (p. 127)

"Ifrit at Blue Spring, June 1987," photo by Nicholas Daniloff, with permission. (p. 132)

"Bungee at Five Weeks, January 1993," photo by Terri Zagrodnick, with permission. (p. 145)

"Alston and Bungee Landing Trout, Len's Lake, July 1999," photo by Michael Simon, with permission. (p. 163)

"From the beginning, Bungee had . . . the loyalty gene," 1995 photo by Tom Murphy, with permission. (p. 166)

"Alston and Hobson, July 2000," photo by Doug Loneman, with permission. (p. 184)

"We flew to Vermont . . ." 2003, photo by David Howe, with permission. (p. 186)

Note: Credit Alston Chase for all other photos.